From Under a Dark Cloud

Deb McGregor-Pfleger

With Contributions from Lisa Diekhans,
John Knisley, Jamie Lull, Jamie Kaehler,
Ben Mettling and P.J. Ziegler

First printing, October 2006 by Richards Publishing P.O. Box 159, Gonvick, MN 56644.

Copyright 2006 by Deb McGregor-Pfleger

All rights reserved. No part of this book may be used or reproduced in any manner whatsoever without written permission, except in the case of reprints in the context of reviews.

ISBN-13: 978-0-9759180-3-6
ISBN-10: 0-9759180-3-6

Scripture texts in this work are taken from the *New American Bible with Revised New Testament* © 1986, 1970 Confraternity of Christian Doctrine, Washington, D.C. and are used by permission of the copyright owner. All Rights Reserved. No part of the *New American Bible* may be reproduced in any form without permission in writing from the copyright owner.

All efforts have been made to recount this testimony as accurately as possible. Any discrepancies are not intentional.

The author and printing company have sought to obtain the copyright holder's permission and to give proper acknowledgement for the prayers, poems, and stories that appear in this book. To the best of our knowledge, anything not credited is in the public domain. If through inadvertence a copyright has not been acknowledged, sincere apologies are offered with the assurance that this omission will be corrected in any future edition.

Cover and back design by Joni Armstrong.

Photos submitted by the author and team members, except for the photos on p. 18, 19, 24, 41, 50, 53, 64, 91, 96, 103, 104 and 123, which were taken by Rebecca Nelson.

Printed and bound in the United States of America.

Dedications

This book is dedicated to the following people without whom I wouldn't be the person that God intended me to be.

God: *You are so good and without You I am nothing. Thank you for Your grace and all of the forgiveness You have given me as well as the trust You have given me to do Your will. You told me that You wanted me to complete this book and go out and share its message. I hope I have completed the project as You wanted me to do it. I am humbled that You would choose to work through me to accomplish such a big task but I stand ready to continue to do Your will. Praise You Lord!*

Mother Mary: *You gave us your Son, who came to this world to die for our sins. Only a mother can imagine the pain and sorrow you must have had watching your Son be crucified so that the rest of us can be forgiven of our sins. You know the importance of peace, fasting, penance and prayer. Thank you for reminding us of these messages and thank you for being our mother. Your grace has served as such an inspiration for me. I thank you for sharing that grace and I thank you for being one I can turn to for intercession to our Lord, Jesus Christ.*

My husband Stephen: *You deserve 100 gold medals for all the support you have given me. You are more than I ever could have wanted in a husband—you* *are my best friend and my partner for life. You are such a wonderful gift to our children and me. Thank you for your commitment to our marriage and this project. I know it has meant so many sacrifices for you. Thank you for your willingness to listen to God's plan for us. For the many times you had to listen to yet another part of this plan, I am grateful. Your trust and confidence in me is overwhelming. Thank you for all the warm meals and clean home. You are the best!*

Madeleine and Ryan: *You are both the greatest gifts from God! What an incredible responsibility He gives us when we become parents! I love all of the hugs, kisses and snuggles we have every day! You are both such a joy to be around and I pray that God continues to bless you with many gifts and that you use those gifts to do His will. Thank you for understanding mommy's commitment to doing God's will by completing this book for Him.*

My parents, brother and sister: *Thank you for always providing a stable home and all of the wonderful opportunities we had growing up. This foundation has proven to be the source of so many gifts that God is now using to complete His will and plan for me. Mom and dad—I will always respect the trust and integrity with which you made decisions. While I may not have always been happy at the time, I respect your following of the Ten Commandments and see that you were doing what God asked you to do.*

Bec: *I have always thought of you as my "other sister". You have always been like one of our family. You have been there to celebrate the joys and wipe away the tears. You have always been willing to "say it like it is" when it needed to be done. You are a true friend and I have been so blessed to have you in my* life. Thank you for the many chats and keeping me focused. Your words of encouragement and support are so appreciated!

Shel: *Thank you for praying for me when I was still in a big fog. I am convinced that through the prayers of you as well as a few others, I eventually came to Christ's light. I am so grateful for every word of prayer that was spoken. We have shared so many things together—some struggles and a lot of joy. I appreciate every moment of both. As you know, we sometimes learn more in the struggle than in the joy! Blessings for the future!*

Ben: *Words cannot describe the incredible gratitude I have for you and your willingness to answer God's call to help me. You are the one who has endured hours of listening and processing with me. It was all done without hesitation on your part. You taught me how to trust again and have faith in other people. You taught me how to "go with the flow". You were there when I needed someone to listen in a way that most people cannot comprehend. You were there to help me go through a process of forgiveness that the majority of people couldn't do in their lifetime—not because of time but because of the strength and courage that it takes. You helped give me that strength and you helped me find the courage. Just knowing you were there supporting me was sometimes all I needed to keep moving forward. You kept me grounded and focused when it was necessary. The most amazing thing to me is that I still don't think you realize how much of an impact you have been throughout this journey. You have been the rock, and without that rock, I may still have been out floating somewhere. The journey with you has definitely been "way up there"!*

P.J.: *To "my" Olie-I will never forget the first time we walked into the weight room together or walked the track and had "the talk". You were my constant at the beginning of this journey and I am so grateful for all of the time you took with me to help ensure my success. We shared so many great moments in the gym, work and our home. Your encouragement and support kept me going when I didn't think I had another step left in me. The strength you showed in your faith was such a strong example to me. There were times that you believed in me when I didn't believe in myself. After all of this, I think it's time to put this book "on the board". YEAH!*

Jamie K: *Well, Bad Monkey, you have certainly earned the title of "girlfriend" in my book. You are an amazing woman and I thank God that you and I were brought together. You smile and I smile. You warm my heart. There have been so many great lunches, dinners, stories and prayer sessions shared. I feel so blessed that you were willing to answer God's call to be on this team. When God revealed you to me, I knew He knew what He was doing. It is an honor and privilege to have you on this journey. I have appreciated every phone call and e-mail that we've exchanged. I am grateful for your phone being turned on at all hours, so in my moments of struggle, I knew you were there to call. I am also so glad that being on this journey with me has also brought you closer to our Lord. You are a Woman of God and I am looking forward to doing more of God's work with you in the future.*

John: *From the moment I took the kayak course, I knew there would be a place for you on this team. As we got to know each other over many cups of coffee, I realized that not only would you be good for this team but that the team would be really good for you. I had* *a soul connection with you that was unexplainable for so long but as we got to know each other, it became so much clearer. God brought us together for a reason and it has been through this team that His plan was revealed. Thank you for the many incredible prayer sessions, sharing of yourself and most importantly, your willingness to return to God, so you, too, could do His will.*

Lisa: *We've been friends since elementary school and I am so grateful we remain friends today. Your return to Christ and your intercessory prayers for me is what got me back on track and gave me the ability to begin a healing journey that I don't think either of us ever could have imagined. You answered God's call and through your willingness to do this, you have touched so many people's lives. You are an evangelist! I cannot thank you enough for your willingness to let God work through you to reach me. You are awesome!*

Jamie L: *God's Armor for God's Glory—so many times we have used that phrase with each other. It is so true. Thank you for coming into my life at a time when I needed your commitment to doing God's work at any price. Thank you for constantly reminding me of the next world and doing everything in God's name. There are so many times that I can remember the uplifting you did for me and often, it was your words that assisted me in moving on to the next step. Thank you for always looking for individuals who needed to hear the message. There are so many who have come to know our Lord through the work that both of us did together and there will be many more to come! Praise His name!*

Cathy: *Thank you for being such a great friend! I appreciate the fact that you were praying for me in some* *of my darker moments. I am so grateful that each of us is continuing to grow in faith and I value each and every conversation we have shared, especially those that have taken place on the bike path. May God's blessings continue to be showered upon you.*

Gary: *You are such a fantastic coach! Thank you for helping me through so many growing points on this journey! I love the way we laugh on our calls. I love the way we've shared tears and I especially enjoy praying with you as we begin our coaching sessions. God has worked through you in a very special way to help bring this book to fruition. You have helped prepare me for God's work and I will always be grateful to you for answering His call! I hope you are rubbing this in!!!*

Tammy: *You are a true friend. I have appreciated the many cups of coffee, tea and shared hours of scrapbooking as we talked about God's plan. You never had a doubt about my completing this project. You have been such a strong, level-headed support throughout this process and I am grateful. I value all of the trust and confidentiality you have. There is so much more to come and I know you will be a part of it!*

Paulette, Doris and Mary: *Thank you so much for your faith and dedication to Jesus and His mother, Mary. I have learned so much from all of you and it wouldn't have happened if you didn't have such a strong foundation of faith. I appreciate every prayer you've ever said for me and every Mass you have requested. You have really assisted me in doing God's work and I am so grateful. I know there will be a lot more work to accomplish together!*

Barb: *You have been the "wisdom" for me so many times. When I had doubts, you took away the fear and* *encouraged me to keep going. When I had tears, you wiped them away. When I talked, you listened. So many times, you had the answers I needed. I thank you for your wisdom and willingness to be a part of this journey. I love you!*

Rollin: *Thank you for the discussion in the café. Who would have thought that the discussion we had would have led to all the incredible things that have taken place in our lives. Thank you for always believing in me, always cheering me on, supporting me and most of all, never letting me down. You are an incredible human being!*

Joni: *God has given you some amazing gifts! One of the gifts He has given you for this project is your artistic ability! Thank you for such a beautiful cover and back design that illustrates the feelings within this book. Your ability to pick out some great Bible verses is also appreciated. I am grateful for every prayer you have ever said for me.*

Laurie, John and Lyndsay: *Thank you for helping me in so many ways. I have appreciated every discussion and e-mail. You have helped "fill in the blanks" when it was necessary. I am grateful for all the meals, warm showers and encouragement. Laurie and John—most of all, thank you for having your son, Ben, who has been such an instrumental part of my journey.*

Father Joe: *Thank you so much for your patience and gentleness with my return to Reconciliation. Thank you for the hours spent talking about this project and God's will for me. I will always remember the moment when we both saw Jesus in your photo. What a gift to both of us! I also appreciate all that you have* *shared with me! I feel so blessed to have shared such a special sacrament with you!*

Father Bill: *I am so glad that God revealed you to me so that we both had the opportunity to know each other and share God's love. I am grateful for you bringing Sister Teresa of Avila to my attention. This definitely lead to a much bigger understanding of some of God's "mystical" gifts. You are such a beautiful person and I feel blessed to know you. Thank you for sharing your homilies in the books you wrote. Your commitment to social justice is refreshing and I appreciate the fact that you are answering God's call for you.*

Father Antony: *What a gift you are! God put you in the right place at the right time! Our conversation regarding the Holy Spirit and how He moves within each one of us was incredible. I know that God put us in each other's path to both reinforce the presence of the Spirit working within people and to encourage us to continue to do more to keep that Spirit flowing. I am grateful for the many times that the Holy Spirit worked through you to reach both my husband and me.*

Father Todd: *Thank you for the many times you have let God work through you to reach me with important messages. Whether it was your homily, comments at Reconciliation or in simple conversation, God was able to communicate to me through you and this was often something that kept me moving to the next step. While your time at St. Philip's was very short, I am so honored to have worked with you during this time and to have benefited from your decision to be a priest. Thank you!*

Father Vincent: *Thank you for your openness*

to this book and the mission trip. Thank you for recognizing my personal commitment to prayer and the answers that only come through prayer. Your calmness and ability to listen are much appreciated. I know God has big plans in store for you and I am honored to have been called to be one of the individuals praying for you.

Father Charlie: *Thank you for writing your book, Raising Roger's Cross. Thank you for your commitment to share stories of the cross. Thank you for returning my phone call when I was just starting this book and didn't know where to go with it. Thank you for the encouraging e-mails and all the help along the way. I am grateful for your willingness to help me in getting this book written, edited and published.*

Pastor Stan: *Thank you for meeting with me as I was beginning the start of my mission work. It was an awesome meeting. You helped me realize what a powerful message it is that no matter what our "denomination", we, as Christians are spreading the word of Jesus Christ. His love, His forgiveness, His grace are celebrated by all of us and this is the incredible gift He gave us when He died on the cross. I was so blessed by our conversation.*

Pastor Mark: *Thank you for an incredible meeting that was totally driven by the Holy Spirit. You helped me see a much bigger picture with this message and you also helped me realize the many different ways that this message will impact people. Thank you so much for your belief in God's work that is being accomplished through this book.*

Mike: *Thank you for wanting to help God and me with the scriptural passages in the book. When I shared* *my story with you, I appreciated your insight, questions and sincere desire to understand. Thank you for your commitment to doing God's work as a profession.*

Rabi: *Thank you for your trust and friendship. I am grateful for our conversation on the bike path and know that it was an instrumental part of healing for both of us. You are definitely a light in this world. I have enjoyed every bike ride and every conversation we've shared. Thank you for being you. I am so blessed to know you.*

Laura: *God has definitely brought us together for His purpose! I am so glad you have found Christ's light and I am so grateful for your willingness to answer His call too! You are such a unique and special gift to the world. Thank you for listening to me and helping me process throughout this journey.*

James: *Thank you for all of the hard work in helping me to get this book printed! You do amazing work and I am so grateful for the "extra" you put into everything you do! I also enjoyed our conversations about being a Christian and how God works in our lives. I am grateful that we knew each other well enough that I was very comfortable in trusting you with this project! God put you in my path for a reason!*

Bikers in Training: *Each one of you has been such an awesome gift and your support has been amazing! Thanks for all the great bike rides, talks and snacks! Hats off to Steve, Kelly, Jessie Lynn, Noemi, Al, Carol, Harry, Kim, Jenn, Trista, Kelli, Rabi and Ben for all the biked miles! Bike On!*

Contents

PROLOGUE
15

INTRODUCTION
17

Section I—The Start and Background
19

CHAPTER ONE
P.J. "Olie"
20

CHAPTER TWO
The Turn From God
24

Section II-The People and Experiences throughout the Conversion
41

CHAPTER THREE
Lisa "The Quiet Evangelist"
42

CHAPTER FOUR
The Miracle Hour
50

CHAPTER FIVE
The Holy Spirit
53

CHAPTER SIX
Ben "Rubberband Man"
56

CHAPTER SEVEN
Jamie K "Bad Monkey"
64

CHAPTER EIGHT
The Existence of Satan
78

CHAPTER NINE
Forgiving Others
91

CHAPTER TEN
Medjagorge
96

CHAPTER ELEVEN
A New Rape Victim
104

CHAPTER TWELVE
John "A Man of Nature"
107

CHAPTER THIRTEEN
Return to Reconciliation
123

CHAPTER FOURTEEN
Jamie L "Armor Man"
130

Section III-The Future
140

CHAPTER FIFTEEN
The Team
141

EPILOGUE
145

RESOURCES
148

PROLOGUE

This book is about my conversion story. This book covers the reason why I turned my back on God in the first place, what life was like during this time of darkness and what life is like today since surrendering myself to God's will. To follow this story more easily, this book is divided into three sections: the start of the story and background information; people and experiences throughout the conversion; and the future-what happens next. It is important to note that one of the unique components of this conversion process has been the individuals whom God has brought to me as a part of my healing. These individuals have formed a team unlike any other that I have ever seen elsewhere and most definitely had not, up until this point, experienced myself. For this reason, I have specifically identified members throughout the book as well as provided an opportunity for each of them to contribute to the book. God has inspired each of them to be involved in this healing process and it is my hope that they will inspire you as well.

In some of the sections, you will also find:

Scripture Passages: Scripture passages that reinforce the message of each chapter. This provides an opportunity for the reader to reflect on the real life story and how it ties into a message from scripture.

Points to Ponder: These are questions to ask yourself after you've read the chapter. It will provide an opportunity for additional reflection and an opportunity to make the story more real for you, the reader.

Team Member's Stories: This is an opportunity for the team members who've been involved in this story to share their perspective, strength and hope. Team members have inserted their thoughts where they felt it would enhance the story and meaning in the book.

You are the light of the world. A city set on a hill cannot be hidden. Men do not light a lamp and then put it under a bushel basket. They set it on a stand where it gives light to all in the house. In the same way, your light must shine before men so that they may see goodness in your acts and give praise to your heavenly Father.
Matthew 5:14-16

To me, the least of all believers, was given the grace to preach to the Gentiles the unfathomable riches of Christ and to enlighten all men on the mysterious design which for ages was hidden in God, the Creator of all. Now, therefore, through the church, God's manifold wisdom is made known to the principalities and powers off heaven. In accord with his age-old purpose, carried out in Christ Jesus our Lord. In Christ and through faith in him we can speak freely to God, drawing near him with confidence. Hence, I beg you not to be disheartened by the trials I endure for you; they are your glory.
Ephesians 3: 8-13

I repeat, it is owing to his favor that salvation is yours through faith. This is not your own doing, it is God's gift; neither is it a reward for anything you have accomplished, so let no one pride himself on it. We are truly his handiwork, created in Christ Jesus to lead the life of good deeds which God prepared for us in advance.
Ephesians 2: 8-10

INTRODUCTION

Journeys.. the concept of a journey brings different images to each of us but I like to think of a journey as a series of steps that get us to where we are supposed to be. Some journeys are short and some are long. I used to think that journeys had a definite starting and ending point. After going through this experience, I see that some journeys are meant to be ongoing. Some journeys happen quickly, some last a lifetime. One thing I have learned is that journeys are meant to teach us things—we learn from every step of the journey and it is through this learning that we grow and become the person we are supposed to be and doing the things we are supposed to do. For me, the conversion to truly doing God's work has been an incredible journey—the people I've met, the things I've learned, the mistakes I've made, the sorrows, the joys, the laughter and the tears—it is all of these things that have made this journey the adventure of a lifetime. I hope you enjoy reading about and learning from this adventure as much as I continue to enjoy living it.

From Under a Dark Cloud

I look up to the sky and a dark cloud is rolling over me. I feel afraid. I feel scared. I feel alone. The rain starts falling and I begin to cry uncontrollably. I feel lost. Where am I? Is there anyone out there? It is so dark and empty. But hope comes... through a friend comes a distant prayer and the rain starts to dwindle. I'm not lonely anymore. I'm not afraid. I am calm. I have peace. I look up—the sky is clearing and the clouds are breaking. I see light.. God's light.. and I know everything will be all right. I am once again in His arms—safe and protected from the darkness.

There was a time when you were darkness but now you are light in the Lord. Well, then, live as children of light. Light produces every kind of goodness and justice and truth. Be correct in your judgment of what pleases the Lord. Take no part in vain deeds done in darkness; rather, condemn them.
Ephesians 5: 8-11

SECTION I—The Start and Background

In the beginning, when God created the heavens and the earth, the earth was a formless wasteland, and darkness covered the abyss, while a mighty wind swept over the waters. Then God said, "Let there be light," and there was light. God saw how good the light was. God then separated the light from the darkness. God called the light "day," and the darkness he called "night." Thus evening came, and morning followed—the first day.
Genesis 1: 1-5

CHAPTER ONE

P.J.
"Olie"

I didn't wake up one morning and say, "oh, today I am giving myself to Christ." It wasn't that simple. In fact, it wasn't like that at all. What really happened is that I woke up one morning and said, "I have got to get into better shape and get back into the gym." I knew that I was hiding behind my weight and it was time to deal with the issues surrounding my weight problem. I knew that it would be no small task and that I would need help. I prayed for God to bring people to me who could help. For some reason, I felt directed to a co-worker who I knew lifted weights at the local recreational center. One day, I finally got up the courage to call him and ask him for help. I think the call was something like this, "P.J., hi, it's Deb from Development. I know you don't know me very well and I'm really nervous to make this phone call, but I was wondering if you would be willing to help me in the weight room." I could feel my heart beating and what I heard was "sure, I'd love to help you get started—when do you want to get going?" I said, "well,

I was thinking that the middle of September would be good." "Great," he said. " I'll send you some helpful information in the meantime." I didn't know it at the time, but P.J. became the first official member of my team. He also became one of my strongest supporters and cheerleaders.

On September 14th, P.J. and I met in the weight room. It took every ounce of courage I had to walk with him into the weight room. I looked in the mirror and saw that I was as pale as a ghost. P.J. asked me if I was all right. I told him that I was and that this was such a huge step for me. He proceeded to show me the routine and we made lots of notations on a sheet he had provided me that listed all the different "lifting" exercises that I should be doing. We met for the next few days until I was comfortable with the routine. At that point, I was ready to do it on my own. I wasn't 100% confident, but I knew I had the tools to make it happen. I sent P.J. an e-mail thanking him for his time. I told him that he had no idea how big of a deal this was to me. I expressed my gratitude to him. At the time, he had no comprehension of the importance of getting into the weight room. It wasn't until I told him about "the incident" that he fully understood the magnitude of stepping into that weight room and taking this step. It was life changing.

P.J.'s Corner:

As a wise man once said, to get ahead in life you need to lie, cheat, drink and steal. Okay, now that I have your attention let me explain. Lie: Lie back and relax just a little more and let a little more life happen to you without so much worry. Cheat: Cheat failure. Don't be afraid to try something new because you think you may fail. It is through failure that we learn the most valuable lessons. Drink: Drink from the fountain of knowledge. Many people around you have already been down roads you are about to travel. Learn from mistakes they have made. Take what they have learned and use it. And finally, Steal: Steal a little time for God. Everyday take a little more time to develop your relationship with the man above.

The lie, cheat, drink and steal motto is one I live by daily and it's one that came so true on that September afternoon when Deb McGregor-Pfleger called me from her office and asked me to help her get started on a weight lifting program. At first, I was shocked and didn't know how to respond for the simple fact that I never really knew Deb that well except for the times we spent at work, working. I didn't really know how much of an impact I would make. To be honest, I did not think it would last long. But then I remembered the motto, lie, cheat, drink and steal and I thought this would be a great opportunity to cheat failure and drink from the fountain of knowledge. So in Mid-September, Deb and I met in the weight room and our journey down a long and winding road began. Our friendship started to grow and with every little step, we got further and further down the road-less traveled. I didn't know that taking 20 minutes out of my day that September afternoon would change somebody's life forever. I would come to realize that getting back in the weight room for Deb was such a small step in her life, but a big step into the person she always wanted to be. To this day, she continues to push herself and others to get stronger both in the weight room and in life. I am so glad I took the time, the chance and the opportunity. I hope one day when someone asks you for 10 minutes of your time you think about lying, cheating, drinking and stealing and remember it only takes one person to change a life forever. As an unknown author once wrote: to the world, you may be just one person, but to just one person, you may be the world. God Bless.

Help carry one another's burdens; in that way you will fulfill the law of Christ.
  Galatians 6:2

While we have the opportunity, let us do good to all men—but especially those of the household of the faith.
  Galatians 6:10

He sins who despises the hungry; but happy is he who is kind to the poor!
  Proverbs 14:21

Because you are God's chosen ones, holy and beloved, clothe yourselves with heartfelt mercy, with kindness, humility, meekness, and patience.
  Colossians 3:12

Points to Ponder:

Has someone ever asked you for help?

How did you respond?

How does it feel to help someone in need?

What does God tell us about helping others in need?

Is there someone that you can think of right now that needs your help?

CHAPTER TWO

The Turn From God

So what is it that happened that made me turn away from God in the first place? That is really where this story begins and it's important that I share it with you so you can truly understand where it all began, why I turned away from God and how long of a process it has been to get to where I am today. Understanding this will also help you see how each of the individuals in this book has helped me heal and truly be able to live in the love of Christ. It is my hope that if you are reading this book and in need of healing, you will receive hope and encouragement as well as ideas of how to move forward in that healing. If you are not in need of this healing, you may be in a position to help someone who is. By learning how others helped me, you, in turn, may be able to visualize yourself helping someone else.

I'd like to take you back to January of 1985. It was a typical winter in Montana. Not too much snow-the Chinook winds normally take care of that. I was probably a fairly typical teenager. I was involved in many things—I was a competitive swimmer, active in student government, choir, Girls State, National Honor Society and much more depending on the time of year. I was also a good student. People would describe me as funny, energetic, caring and talented. I was also very committed to my Catholic faith. I believed very strongly in "waiting until I was married" and looked forward to the day when I would have a husband and children with whom I could share this strong commitment to faith. In so many ways, I had everything going for me. It is amazing how quickly everything can change, however. For me, the change took place over a four-hour period. I do want to let you know that if you are uncomfortable with reading the details that follow, feel free to skip over this part. My intent with putting the details in here isn't to cause any pain or do it for shock value but rather it is so you can understand the depth and horrors of rape. I want you to understand how rape robs a person emotionally, physically and spiritually. I also want you to understand how being betrayed by people you thought were your friends can scar you for many years. I also want to make sure that you read until the end of the book because you will see how God uses everything, even this rape, for His good. It may be difficult to see or accept that at first and it has taken me many years to see it, but now I do and understand how God wants me to share this story with you so His will can be done.

A girlfriend invited me to go out and play cards with a group of her friends. It sounded like fun, so I said sure. We went to her friend's house and played cards.

I had met one of the individuals before, but everyone else was new to me. After we finished playing cards, we were going to get up and leave. As I was getting up and moving towards the door, one of the guys pushed me down. I said, "hey, what are you doing? Stop playing around." I tried to get up and he pushed me back down. This time he got on top of me and started holding my hands down. I said, "stop it, you're hurting me" and he told me to shut up. I looked at my girlfriend and the other guys and said, "aren't you going to do anything to help me?" They just shrugged their shoulders at me. I had no idea what was going on. The guy started trying to kiss me and then ripped open my shirt. I said, "no, stop!" He kept saying, "you know you want it." I said, "no, I don't, please stop." I was absolutely terrified. At this point, he started unzipping my jeans and pulling down my pants. I started screaming. He put his hand over my mouth and told me to be quiet. I bit his hand. That made him angry. He called me a bitch and pulled down my underwear. This entire time, my girlfriend and the other guys were standing there watching. They were laughing and cheering him on. I just looked over at them with tears in my eyes and couldn't understand why they wouldn't help me. The guy grabbed a blanket and threw it over me and he forced himself in me. Since I was a virgin and because it was forced, it didn't just hurt emotionally, it hurt physically too. I was bleeding all over. When he finished, he said, "that was good you fuckin' bitch-we should do this again sometime." I wanted to throw up. After he got off of me, I made my way to the bathroom and tried to pull myself together. I was trying to figure out how to get home knowing that I had been betrayed by my girlfriend. She came into the bathroom and started talking to me. I realized in our discussion that this nightmare wasn't over. The other three guys who were there wanted to have their fun too. The plan was that they were taking me to another place. I looked at my girlfriend in desperation. Couldn't she call for help? What was going on? Why was this happening? I walked out of the bathroom and the other three guys were waiting for me. They took my arms and said that I was going with them. "Where are we going?" I asked. I told them I just wanted to go home. They told me that I had to go with them and after we were done, I could go home. At this point, I didn't know what to do. Running wasn't an option. I knew the three of them would have me tackled in no time. I couldn't call for help because they were with me. If this happened in today's world, I probably would have had a cell phone and could have made a call for help in the bathroom. I knew I was trapped and it was a horrible feeling. I also felt set up. So many questions were on my mind and unfortunately, there weren't any answers.

At this point, the three guys took me to another house. I didn't know what to expect, but I knew it wasn't going to be good. I am not going to go into all of the details here, but it is important to know that I was there for at least four hours and I was raped by all three of them in almost every way that you can imagine. There were a couple times when I knew they knew that what they were doing was wrong. At one point, one of the guys was trying to rape me and he was struggling. I was just staring at him with the tears streaming down my face. I could see the tears welling up in his eyes too. Finally, he just stopped and told the next guy to take his turn. By the time they finished, I was very sore. I could barely walk. I remember making my way out of the house and trying to figure out where I was. I realized that I was near a friend's home and I called her to come and pick me up at a church that was close by. She did pick me up and I made her promise not to tell my parents or call the cops. In fact, I tried to downplay everything and attempted to convince her and myself that I couldn't possibly have been raped. These kinds of things don't happen, especially in our town. She was insistent that we should do something. I told her that I didn't want to tell my parents because I knew how upset and hurt they would be that this had happened. The guys had also threatened me and my family if I called the cops. I knew that if my parents knew, they would call the cops. I knew that if the cops were called, they'd catch the guys and they would send someone after my family and me. I just decided that the best thing to do was just forget it.

If, however, it is in the open fields that a man comes upon such a betrothed maiden, seizes her and has relations with her, the man alone shall die. You shall do nothing to the maiden, since she is not guilty of a capital offense. This case is like that of a man who rises up against his neighbor and murders him: it was in the open fields that he came upon her, and though the betrothed maiden may have cried out for help, there was no one to come to her aid.
Deuteronomy 22:25-27

Leave it to the Lord, and wait for Him; Be not vexed at the successful path of the man who does malicious deeds.
Psalm 37:7

The Lord confronts the evildoers, to destroy remembrance of them from the earth. When the just cry out, the Lord hears them, and from all their distress he rescues them. The Lord is close to the brokenhearted; and those who are crushed in spirit he saves.
Psalm 34: 17-19

He kept saying, "Abba, you have the power to do all things. Take this cup away from me. But let it be as

you would have it, not as I."
Mark 14: 36

I received from the Lord what I handed on to you, namely, that the Lord Jesus on the night in which he was betrayed too bread, and after he had given thanks, broke it and said, "This is my body, which is for you. Do this in remembrance of me."
Corinthians 11:23-24

While he was still speaking, Judas, one of the Twelve, arrived accompanied by a great crowed with swords and clubs. They had been sent by the chief priests and elders of the people. His betrayer had arranged to give them a signal, saying, "The man I shall embrace is the one; take hold off him." He embraced him. Jesus answered, "Friend, do what you are here for!" At that moment they stepped forward to lay hands on Jesus, and arrested him.
Matthew 26: 47-50

Points to Ponder:

Have you ever been raped or know someone who has been raped?

Where are you in your healing process?

What further action do you need to do to heal?

Have you ever been betrayed? How did that make you feel?

Have you ever betrayed someone else? Have you asked for forgiveness?

I spent most of the next week crying. I had run into one of the guys at school and he told me how much fun they'd had and how we should do it again sometime. I had to run to the bathroom. I thought I was going to throw up on the spot. I also had a lot of physical wounds. My arms and neck were covered with so many marks that I wore turtlenecks for a while so they would be covered up. You may be surprised that no one noticed. Our family was so busy at the time that I honestly think we were in a mode of automatic pilot. We were in the process of building a house and we were living at my grandpa's house. We barely saw each other and I made myself pretty scarce. In addition, I started drinking heavily, as in almost every day. It was the only way that I could avoid the pain of what had happened. Getting money wasn't an issue and finding people to buy alcohol was very easy. I also found people who would drink before school. I started leaving about 30-45 minutes before school so I could "relax" a little before school. I would also put vodka in a closed mug and keep it in my locker. This usually kept me fairly steady all day. I started to have some challenges in school. I got the first "D" that I've ever gotten in my life. I remember the teacher calling me up to the front of the classroom and asking me if my parents would be upset because I was getting a "D". There was no concern about what was going on and why my grades were slipping but the concern was about how my parents would react. I was absolutely dying inside but no one knew the reason. During this time period, I was going to church, but I don't think I even heard a word. I was so angry with God for letting this happen that I didn't want to hear anything about Him or what I should do for Him. He let me down. I understood the importance of God asking us to wait to have sex until we were married and now I had been raped not by just one, but four men. What did that mean for me? Was I even worthy of getting married? I decided that no man would probably want to marry me after what had happened any way. The more I thought about all of this, the more depressed I got. The more depressed I got, the more I drank. Eventually, the drinking caught up with me and my aunt told my parents about the amount of alcohol I had been consuming. At this point, I thought that I must be an alcoholic. I was drinking every day and it was definitely a problem. What I know now is that I'm not an alcoholic but that I used the alcohol as a coping mechanism at that time. My parents turned me into the school as they had signed a contract that said if your child is caught drinking, they should be turned into the school for probation. I was involved in choir very extensively and had to go on probation for that. I also had to take part in an "intervention" program. This involved sessions of alcohol awareness and counseling. At the time, I really thought I had an alcohol problem. I remember being worried that my parents wouldn't accept me anymore. My dad was convinced that I wasn't an alcoholic and that I just had a "self-discipline" problem. I still didn't have the heart to tell him about the real reason that I was always drinking. My parents also decided to send me to "Search", which is a religious retreat for high school age kids. I know that I felt something at the retreat but I was in so much pain that it didn't get to my core. There were so many kids who were in pain at that retreat. I remember feeling so down about how many problems are out there and how helpless I felt to do anything about it. I also remember being so depressed when my family came to pick me up. In the Search group, I felt safe and enclosed by God's loving arms but the minute we departed, I felt like I walked right back into the darkness of the life I'd left for a couple of days. There was a good thing that came out of the Search and that was meeting Steve (not my husband), who ended up being the friend and eventually boyfriend that I needed at this stage in my life. Steve had been involved in many Searches and I was very attracted to his fun loving spirit. He was also a good listener and friend, which is what I so desperately needed at this stage. After making a connection through friends, Steve and I started dating. We became very close. I did tell him about everything including the rape. He was a good support system and did his best to help me through it. Of course, neither one of us really knew how to deal with it on a bigger scale, but at least, for the time being, I wasn't drinking and I had someone with whom I could share the pain.

In the fall of 1986, I headed off to college. Steve and I were still dating, but we started to have some challenges being so far away. In addition, he enlisted in the military, which made seeing each other even more difficult. Being away was difficult for me. I felt so alone so many times and I often struggled just to hang in there. In addition, an incident happened on campus that once again, continued to turn me away from God. A male friend and I had gone to a lounge to eat pizza and watch an "oldie but goodie" movie. When it was almost done, he decided to go up to bed. I really wanted to watch the end of the movie, so I decided to stay and finish it. About 10 minutes or so after he left, another guy, who had obviously been drinking, came into the lounge. He tried to make a move on me. I told him that I had a boyfriend and wasn't interested. He left. I wasn't worried and continued to watch the movie. A few minutes later, he returned, although this time he wasn't being polite. He picked me up and threw me against a chair. He was incredibly strong. He had me pinned up against the chair and was trying to unzip my pants. I was screaming for help and he bit my neck. I had a mark on my neck for a good month. I started praying for someone, something to intervene. All of a sudden, I heard footsteps. I screamed again and this time, the guy got up and started leaving. I think he heard someone coming too. I ran out and ran into a guy coming down the stairs. At that point, he looked like a "Savior" to me. He ended up helping me out of the lounge and up towards my dorm. It took me three days to get up the courage to call Security but I did. They interviewed the guy and me several times. He kept changing his story. The reality was, he was probably so drunk, he didn't even remember attacking me. I took him to court on campus. They found him guilty of a "lesser charge" but still guilty. At least this time, I did something about it. I still can't believe that this happened but I had learned from the first time. My parents came out to support me and they were very helpful. The hard part was dealing with all the gossip on campus. People would make comments to me or blame me for what had happened. Since when is eating pizza and watching a movie on campus a crime? The doubt about God was starting again. I could see that He had sent someone to help me but I was consumed with the "why" it happened and all of the harassment I was taking on campus. Again, the pain was so great and I just didn't have a good place to turn. Unfortunately, it was somewhere in here that I was introduced to a couple of people who were involved in satanic worship. I don't want people to get freaked out when they read this part because to many people, just saying the word satan gets them scared. People should be scared because satan is real and he will try and do anything he can to get in the way of God's plan and purpose for each one of us. Satan tries to remain hidden and rarely reveals his true self, which is why most people don't recognize his presence. There are some who don't even want to talk about satan. Guess what? If you don't talk about him, he isn't going away. He is still here. In fact, it allows him to move around more freely and do his evil work. People need to be informed and they need to have their guard up. This is serious stuff. The reason I want you to read the next part is so you can understand a little more about how he tries to infiltrate so that you can not only protect yourself but so you can protect others around you. It started with something as simple as tarot cards. If you aren't familiar with tarot cards, they are used to predict events or tell us about specific things. These are not used for God's purpose and it is not God working through the cards—it is satan and his evil spirits. Anytime we take our focus off of God and provide a means for evil spirits to enter, it is dangerous territory. Our trust and faith should always be on God—never wavering. Simply speaking, the cards can get addicting and they can be used to go against God's will. The same is true of Ouiji boards. It is satan making the letters appear—it is not God. There are so many young kids who are "innocently" playing with the Ouiji board and inadvertently invite evil spirits into their lives. This is one of the tricks that satan uses. The kids think it's cool and that they have some special power—the ONLY true power comes from God—NOT a Ouiji board. From these types of games, people get hooked. They want to know more and want to be able to do more. It becomes mystical in many ways—but not mystical for God's work, mystical for the other side. One very dangerous game is the calling up of dead spirits. There is a difference to note here. Spiritism is the calling up of the spirits by an individual. This is not God's work. There are times in prayer when God will allow a spirit to come to someone. The difference is that when it is God allowing that person through, it is spontaneous and it is not a forced situation. I have been in several prayer sessions where God has allowed a very special person in someone's life to make a presence felt for specific reasons. I have considered these times to be a gift of grace for that individual or myself. I NEVER call upon people myself. I know from experience that it is not something that we should do because we can unintentionally be inviting evil spirits into our bodies. The satanic involvement lasted almost two years. It is something that I find very disgusting as I look back. I was so filled with darkness, that it seemed like a natural place to be. The choices I was making for myself at the time were not good or healthy and I'm not proud of them. I hated myself and I really didn't like anyone around me either. I remember talking with one of my professors who sensed that something was wrong. I told him that someone else was involved with the satanic worship and that I was getting very stressed out about it. I didn't share the fact that I, too, was involved. After I had spoken with him, I remember going back to our apartment and it felt so dark and cold. I knew that our apartment had been infiltrated. I knew I needed to do something. I called my dad and shared a little bit about some of the satanic stuff. He told me that I needed to get out of this apartment. He said something like, "you shouldn't dance with the devil." All I could do was cry. I knew I had made a really serious mistake and I was really worried that it could cost me my soul. My dad called my cousin and her husband to come and pick me up and move all my stuff out. They are very Christian people. We haven't talked about it much but I think that they felt the darkness that was present in the apartment. After we got to their home, I really didn't know what to do. I felt so guilty and yet I wasn't ready to come to the Lord. I know that's what they wanted. I did go to church with them a few times and I know the Lord was trying to call me to Him but I couldn't go. I felt too dark, too dirty. There were too many bad things. How could He forgive me? How could He bestow His grace on me? I knew I wasn't worthy. Did the promises He gave us in the Bible really mean anything? I was so full of confusion that nothing was making sense anymore. I remember going to an event with my cousin and her husband and they did a call for people to come up and pray. I was just sitting in my seat and sobbing. I wanted to go up and be prayed over. I wanted to take a step but it was as if something just kept holding me down in the seat. My body was frozen. I was embarrassed at the thought of having to admit all of these horrible sins to someone else. It was bad enough that I was hiding from God but the thought of sharing this stuff with someone else was absolutely mortifying. Of course, my biggest secret of all was the rape and I knew that once the other stuff started coming out, so would the rape and I definitely wasn't ready to talk about that. So, once again, I chose remaining in the darkness rather than going to God's light and asking for His forgiveness. Even though I was miserable and alone while knowing there was a better choice, I stayed there. About this time, I also met someone who had been a high priestess in a satanic cult. She had been in much deeper than I was. She shared a lot of her stories with me. Fortunately, she had gotten out and by her sharing her stories with me, I knew I definitely didn't want to go back to that type of lifestyle again. I still wasn't in God's light but I had at least departed the horrible darkness that is involved with satanic worship.

After I graduated from college, I returned home. I was still in the process of looking for a job. I started dating a guy who was really bad news. One of the challenges that I really dealt with was my self-esteem. After the rape, I just didn't feel worthy of anyone or anything. I tended to get involved in bad relationships. I thought it was "normal" to be treated poorly and not be respected by a boyfriend. I would always accommodate the person I was dating, even if this meant sacrificing myself. I had such a horrible self-image, that I didn't see myself as attractive in any form. In this particular relationship, I am lucky I survived. This person was both physically and emotionally abusive, not to mention spiritually deprived. Fortunately, God was really looking out for me because I started getting involved in a church. Through that, I met a lady who wanted to set me up with a friend of hers. His name was Stephen. When I met Stephen, I was immediately drawn into his warm personality and caring disposition. He was so nice. I was not used to seeing this quality in the men I had been around. It was so attractive to me. I also liked Stephen's love of life. He was very gentle and had a way with people. He enjoyed talking with me and we shared many conversations. Three years after we met, we were married. It was a lovely ceremony and it was filled with so much joy. I can't say that I had totally accepted God's grace and mercy at this point, but I had at least found love in my husband and I knew he would care and love me in a way that no one else had up to this point. I also knew that he would never physically or emotionally harm me and at this point in my life, that was extremely important. So, I moved into a new chapter of my life—marriage.

Marriage brings a whole new perspective to anyone's world. I think I had my image of what marriage would be and I can honestly say that other than a few things, I was totally wrong about almost every expectation that I had. Marriage is work—it's hard work. There were so many times that it would have been so easy to just give up and walk away, but I loved Stephen and I had made a commitment to him. In addition, there were lots of great times too. The good times outweighed the bad times by far. About five years into our marriage, we had our first child, Madeleine. It was an incredible experience. Bringing life into the world has got to be one of the most important gifts that we are given. I just remember crying and thinking about the miracle that I had helped God with and how that miracle is life. Each one of us is a miracle—God's miracle. Wow—that is a very profound thought. Look at yourself now—you are a miracle—God's creation put here on Earth for a specific purpose.

Children bring a new perspective to marriage. In our case, life became focused on our daughter. The concerns changed and the stresses were different. In addition, I started suffering from horrible post-partum depression. Unfortunately, it went undiagnosed and untreated. Everyone kept telling me that this was normal and it would go away soon. Well, I don't know about normal, but I was very depressed for almost two years. The amazing thing is that I had this beautiful, precious child that I was so in love with, I had a husband whom I loved and he loved me but yet on the inside, I was falling apart. There were days when it took every ounce of energy just to get out of bed. I never felt like I wanted to harm my child in any way, but I did feel hopeless many times and I really didn't know how it would end. Fortunately, it did eventually go away and I actually felt like I was coming out of a fog. It was like life had returned and I could live again.

Life pretty much continued moving forward without any movement from me either towards God or away from God. I was in the middle zone. Three and a half years after Madeleine was born, our son Ryan was born. I was very concerned about having post partum depression again after the experience I had gone through the first time. I had actually spoken with my doctor about it just in case I did get it. Fortunately, I didn't get it with Ryan. In fact, I felt pretty good. Things seemed to fall in place much better and Madeleine adjusted well to having a baby brother. I was still in the middle zone. Stephen and I weren't going to church regularly and always used our kids as an excuse. We didn't want to bring the kids to mass—too much work. We didn't want to go individually because we didn't want to break up the family. The bottom line is that it was all an excuse. We weren't getting any closer to God and we knew it but accepted it. We did have our children baptized as that was very important to us. We kept telling ourselves that when things calmed down, we would get back to church. This was just a transition for us right now. I realize now that this decision to not live in faith or attend church on a regular basis was really keeping us from living fully in Christ's light and sharing His love with others. I wouldn't say we were in total darkness, but we definitely weren't "in the light".

About the time that Madeleine went to Pre-School, I found myself just becoming a very angry and resentful person. Everything around me just seemed to be bothering me. Little things that people did would irritate me. I was very negative. What I didn't know then, that I know now, is that several of my friends were really concerned about me. It turns out that some of my good friends didn't want to hang around me because I had gotten so negative not only about life but about my Catholic faith. I was doubting and questioning everything—but not necessarily in a good way. I was creating doubt within myself and passing on that doubt to other people too. What I have now found out is that during this time, several of these friends began praying for me. It is my belief that these intercessory prayers are eventually what brought me back to God. This should give all of us encouragement. Our prayers do make a difference. Sometimes our prayers are answered instantly and sometimes it may take years, but God does answer our prayers according to His plan for us and others. I continue to be amazed at the power of prayer and have had so many incredible experiences in response to prayer requests. Understanding and doing intercessory prayer has become one of the most important things that I do on a daily basis. We as humans help God in His work when we pray. I used to only do prayers before mealtime and at night. Now, prayer is continuous for me. I not only pray about the things that I am aware of but I also ask God to let me know whom I should be praying for—who needs my prayer assistance each day so that God can accomplish His work. If you are not praying like this, consider trying. Pretty soon, it becomes such a regular part of the day that you don't remember what life was like before you were doing it. Pray on!

SECTION II—The People and Experiences throughout the Conversion

Earlier in the book, I mentioned that God put several people in my life to assist in the conversion process. The next part of this book will introduce some of these individuals as well as experiences in this process. I hope that as you read about each of these individuals, you will see how you may find others around you who can be a part of your healing, or maybe you are supposed to be of service to someone in need.

CHAPTER THREE

Lisa
"The Quiet Evangelist"

My sister got married in October of 2004. Since the wedding was taking place in our hometown, we decided to spend some extra time there and provide additional help for the festivities. While home, I had the opportunity to sit down and talk with my friend

Lisa. Lisa has been my friend since 1st grade. Like all friends, we have definitely had our ups and downs. We went to a Catholic school through 8th grade and were only semi-close in high school. Interestingly enough, both of us had drifted from the church. A few months prior to our meeting, Lisa had started getting more involved with the church again. She was directed to develop a stronger relationship with the Lord and in that process, she had started praying for me. When we met in October, we had a very interesting discussion about the church, its teachings and prayer. Lisa presented me with a book titled *The Miracle Hour* by Linda Schubert. Lisa told me that she had been using this book and it had provided a lot of healing for her. She said she thought I should start praying it too and that maybe I would find some of the healing and answers that I had been seeking. Lisa had also started working with a woman who has a healing ministry. Lisa felt that a lot of her memories had been healed and that as her healing was being done, she was opening up room for God to do His work. This intrigued me. Was it possible that through inner spiritual healing I would be able to release my burdens and free my soul? Was it possible that God was really willing to help me heal so that I could do His work? I made a commitment at that point to start praying *The Miracle Hour*. At the time, I figured that I didn't have anything to lose and that I had a lot to gain. I will also admit that it was somewhat selfish at that point. It wasn't as much about doing God's work as much as it was about healing my own hurts and releasing the pain that was within my heart and soul. Lisa told me that she would continue to pray for me. For some reason this was comforting and I knew that it was important. I thanked her for her courage to talk with me and share *The Miracle Hour*. I decided that Lisa was an evangelist. She isn't the type to speak from a podium or get in front of big groups but in her example and through her actions, she does God's work. God works in mysterious ways at times and little did I know what a turning point this conversation and gift of *The Miracle Hour* would be in my life.

Lisa's Corner:

I first met Debbie McGregor in the first grade. I don't remember much about our early years of friendship. I do, however, remember that Deb was always the leader, and I was the follower. Debbie was the loud one. I was the quiet one. Debbie was always busy, involved in a wide variety of activities at one time. I was content to try one or two. Two more opposite friends there couldn't be. As we grew older, the fights began. We both remember the hair pulling, arm-scratching brawl we had in her basement one day. I think she still has the scars to prove it (as my fingernails were always longer than hers!!). When we began our high school years, we met many new friends and our friendship was put on the back burner.

After high school graduation, Debbie attended college in the Midwest, while I stayed in Montana to attend our state college. Once again, Debbie the go-getter, and I the homebody! We still kept in touch, although sporadically, and would go out together during Christmas vacations. I remember one time Debbie showed her true loyalty as a friend when she visited me in college after a boyfriend broke up with me. She came with her smiling face to cheer me up. It would be one of the many examples of friendship that she has shown me in the 32 years I have known her.

God had a plan for us and He was keeping our friendship alive. We managed to reconnect in the years between college and marriage and were bridesmaids in each others' wedding. Our friendship grew stronger as we began our adjustment to married life and motherhood. We still lived 860 miles apart, but connected through phone calls and Debbie's family vacations back home. Once, when my third child was just born, Debbie came to my house, bearing gifts of lattes and cinnamon rolls! She stated that she would clean while I relaxed. She began to dust...and talk... and talk...and talk.... I don't know how much cleaning she actually accomplished that day, but it was great to have a friend there. Our friendship was now sealed.

Although I had grown up Catholic and attended eight years of parochial school, I felt that my spiritual life was empty. I was a devoted church attendee every Sunday with my husband, Mike, and three children, but I was going out of a sense of obligation. My faith was in my head but not my heart. I had never thought of myself as a spiritual person. In my opinion, praying often, attending daily Mass and praying the rosary was for very religious people and for old widowed women with lots of free time. Sure, I always remembered to ask God for His protection during travel and unsettling times. I usually remembered to say "grace" before meals. I even prayed occasionally for friends' husbands who were in Iraq. But that was the extent of my prayer life. Something was missing.

I could not have imagined that God would want to use someone as quiet, simple and non-religious as I to spread His message of truth. I just wasn't good enough. God would soon show me that He will use anyone who is willing to open their heart to Him. The Holy Spirit must have planted the idea in my heart that I needed a stronger prayer life. I formulated a plan. Each afternoon, when the children were in school and the baby was napping, I would begin a five-minute prayer time. That is all I could do without becoming too bored and sleepy. I was continually distracted by the other things I could be getting done around the house but I kept focusing back onto prayer when I noticed my mind wandering. I also included five minutes of reading the Bible. I even used a timer. What I thought would be a boring history book full of rules was fascinating! God was opening my heart to prayer. My prayer time grew. My spiritual journey was beginning.

A few months later, Mike and I attended the opening of *The Passion of the Christ* movie. I fell in love with the movie and with Jesus. I finally felt in my heart the magnitude of what Jesus had sacrificed for us. I felt joy. I began pouring over the Gospels (the books of Matthew, Mark, Luke and John) and rediscovered things that I had long since forgotten from my Catholic school upbringing. God was removing the scales from my eyes as He had done with Saul/St. Paul, two thousand years earlier. In the next few months, God placed many people in my life to contribute to the transformation process. I began attending a weekly Bible study. I began listening to Christian music on the radio. I developed a friendship with a Catholic friend who instilled in me what true faith really is. I met a true prayer warrior who had stepped out in faith and began her own healing ministry. I began attending monthly confession and felt the burden of past sins lifted off my shoulders. Things were happening in a way that could only be directed by God.

I started calling Debbie more, sometimes twice a week, to tell her all that was happening in my life. For once, I was the talker and she was the listener. She listened with rapt attention to everything I had to say. Her spiritual journey was beginning. I began to pray for Debbie and Stephen, that this new spiritual awakening in her would not cause disunity in their marriage. I prayed that our Almighty God would keep their marriage strong and protect them. I prayed that God would reveal to Debbie what His plan was for her and her family. But most of all, I prayed that the Holy Spirit would give her the gift of discernment so that she would know how to use the special gifts that He was giving her. God is answering those prayers. Praise Jesus!

Many times in my life, I had envied Debbie's ways of always being in the spotlight; wishing that I was more outgoing. I grew up thinking that I would always be a follower - the one to go along with the crowd and follow others' ideas. However, the Holy Spirit helped me realize that I am a leader - a quiet leader. A quiet leader is one who leads by example. One who serves others and the church with humility and without complaint. A quiet leader is one who passes along a good Christian book and recommends that it be read. A quiet leader is one who changes the subject when others start to gossip. A quiet leader is one who says, "I'll pray for you" to the troubled friend.

I have also discovered that being a prayer warrior is a powerful way to be a quiet leader. Prayer does work and Jesus tells us to *"Ask, and you will receive. Seek and you will find. Knock, and it will be opened to you. For the one who asks, receives. The one who seeks, finds. The one who knocks, enters."* Matthew 7:7-8. By praying for others, we open up the doorway so that the Holy Spirit can work in our lives and in those we pray for. I have learned to ask the Holy Spirit daily for guidance in my words, thoughts and actions. God wants us to pray to Him in order to bring us closer to Him. He desires a strong union with us more than we do. Pray for God to fill your heart with

His unfailing love so that you can give that love to others. Pray to see the face of Christ in all you meet. Lastly, pray often for the gifts of the Holy Spirit: wisdom, knowledge, faith, healing, miraculous powers, prophecy, distinguishing between spirits, speaking in tongues, and interpretation of tongues. These are spiritual gifts that God wishes to give us, but we must ask for them.

Conversions are transformations. Sometimes they happen in seconds, as in St. Paul's experience. Mostly, conversions are ongoing and take a lifetime. We must remember that we will not be completely and perfectly transformed until we are dwelling in heaven with our Lord Jesus Christ. I pray that God blesses you abundantly.

Pray perseveringly, be attentive to prayer, and pray in a spirit off thanksgiving. Pray for us, too, that God may provide us with an opening to proclaim the mystery off Christ, for which I am a prisoner. Pray that I may speak it clearly, as I must. Be prudent in dealing with outsiders; make the most of every opportunity.
Colossians 4: 2-5

The man instructed in the word should share all he has with his instructor. Make no mistake about it, no one makes a fool of God! A man will reap only what he sows.
Galatians 6: 6-7

We must consider how to rouse each other to love and good deeds. We should not absent ourselves from the assembly, as some do, but encourage one another; and this all the more because you see that the Day draws near.
Hebrews 10: 24-25

> ### Points to Ponder:
>
> Are you still in contact with classmates from school? Do you ever talk about faith?
>
> Pray for this with whom you went to school. You may be amazed at what happens.

Deb & Lisa at a dinner event.

CHAPTER FOUR

The Miracle Hour

   The Miracle Hour is a little prayer book written by Linda Schubert. This has definitely been a prayer book that has been a big part of the change in my life. *The Miracle Hour* is divided into twelve different sections. The different sections are as follows: praise, sing to the Lord, spiritual warfare, surrender, release of the Holy Spirit, repentance, forgiveness, scripture reflections, wait for the Lord to speak, intercessions, petitions and thanksgiving.

As I started to pray *The Miracle Hour* and spend this quiet time with the Lord, I began to consistently hear from Him. I knew that He wanted to speak to me and through this method of prayer, I was able to open up and hear or feel His words and plan for me. As I began to pray for forgiveness, I started to feel weight lifting off of me. As I prayed for the release of the Holy Spirit, I started to receive gifts from the Holy Spirit. Perhaps one of the strongest gifts I began receiving was the gift of discernment. I was actually able to physically and emotionally feel the presence of evil spirits. One of the most vivid memories I have is of an evening where I was to meet a friend at another woman's home. I arrived at the door and was greeted at the door. My body did not want to enter but I felt a sense of obligation as a guest. When I entered the room, I was immediately surrounded by negative energy and darkness. It was as if this energy were totally trying to consume my thoughts and actions. I actually had to fight to keep my positive, bright light. I left the home as soon as I had the opportunity and I immediately felt the darkness start to lift. The story doesn't stop there. The next morning, I received a call from my friend who proceeded to tell me all the things that her friend didn't like about me and all of the problems I had caused. I was thinking, what problems? I didn't do anything. Her friend had it in for me and tried to create all kinds of problems. I remember calling my parents and telling them that satan was challenging me. This was a test and I needed to let satan know that God would win. I hung in there and tried to stay positive. In the end, the person left me alone and I am happy to report that my friend is no longer "hanging out" with this person on a regular basis. I learned all too quickly that satan's tactics are cunning and he will use anything to try and get to people, especially those who are trying to move closer to doing God's will. Someone once said, "the brighter the light, the darker the shadow" and how true that is. I will never forget that statement and how powerful it is.

Put on the armor of God so that you may be able to stand firm against the tactics of the devil. Our battle is not against human forces but against the principalities and powers, the rulers of this world of darkness, the evil spirits in regions above. You must put on the armor of God if you are to resist on the evil day; do all that your duty requires, and hold your ground. Stand fast, with the trust as the belt around your waist, justice as your breastplate, and zeal to propagate the gospel of peace as your footgear. In all circumstances hold faith up before you as your shield; it will help you extinguish the fiery darts of the evil one. Take the helmet of salvation and the sword of the spirit, the word of God.
Ephesians 6: 11-17

Points to Ponder:

Do you spend quiet time with God each day?

Do you have the gift of discernment? If so, how are you using it? If not, pray a special prayer to the Holy Spirit each day for the gift of discernment.

In what ways does satan have a hold of your life? Pray now to rebuke that hold so that you can be filled entirely with God's love and peace.

CHAPTER FIVE
The Holy Spirit

After I had been praying *The Miracle Hour* for a while, I began to notice something happening. I had always gotten "feelings" about things but never as strong as what was starting to happen with me through this book. I began to have very strong feelings about good and evil spirits. In addition, I was receiving the gift of prophecy at times. I learned later that this would only happen when God wanted me to know something. I began knowing who I should be talking to—who needed a kind word—who needed to be listened to—who needed to be reminded that God existed. It was amazing. One day, I was walking around the track at the Recreational Center and I was praying for the Holy Spirit to enter my life in a bigger way so I could continue to do God's will. After praying about this for about 10 minutes, I felt an incredible gush of wind in my lungs and I couldn't breath. It almost brought me to my knees. My eyes filled with tears. I knew it was the Holy Spirit entering me. I felt an incredible energy—it was as if energy was pulsating through my body. There was a sense of tingling as well. I wanted to shout out in the middle of the Recreational Center that I had just been filled with the Holy Spirit but instead, I got this incredible smile on my face and couldn't take it off. I was so excited and yet scared at the same time. I had a lot of questions.. What does this mean? What do I do with this? Where do I take this? I finally decided that God would direct me with this. I also began praising God and thanking Him for sending His Holy Spirit to be with me so that I could accomplish His work. I finished my workout a lot lighter on my feet and I don't think the smile left my face for quite a long time.

When the day of Pentecost came it found them gathered in one place. Suddenly from up in the sky there came a noise like a strong, driving wind which was heard all through the house where they were seated. Tongues as of fire appeared which parted and came to rest on each of them. All were filled with the Holy Spirit. They began to express themselves in foreign tongues and make bold proclamation as the Spirit prompted them.
Acts 2: 1-4

There are different gifts but the same Spirit; there are different ministries but the same Lord; there are different works but the same God who accomplishes all of them in everyone. To each person the manifestation of the Spirit is given for the common good. To one the Spirit gives wisdom in discourse, to another the power to express knowledge. Through the Spirit one receives faith; by the same Spirit another is given the gift of healing, and still another miraculous powers. Prophecy is given to one; to another power to distinguish one spirit from another. One receives the gift of tongues another that of interpreting the tongues.

But it is one and the same Spirit who produces all these gifts, distributing them to each as he wills.
1 Corinthians, 12: 4-11

That is why I kneel before the Father from whom every family in heaven and on earth takes its name; and I pray that he will bestow on you gifts in keeping with the riches of his glory. May he strengthen you inwardly through the working of his Spirit. May Christ dwell in your hearts through faith, and may charity be the root and foundation of your life.
Ephesians, 4: 14-17

As for myself, brothers, when I came to you I did not come proclaiming God's testimony with any particular eloquence or "wisdom." No, I determined that while I was with you I would speak of nothing but Jesus Christ and him crucified. When I came among you it was in weakness and fear, and with much trepidation. My message and my preaching had none of the persuasive force of "wise" argumentation but the convincing power of the Spirit. As a consequence, your faith rests not on the wisdom of men but on the power of God.
1 Corinthians 2: 1-5

Points to Ponder:

Have you prayed for the release of the Holy Spirit?

Do you let the Holy Spirit provide you with guidance?

What gifts of the Holy Spirit have you received?

How are you using these gifts of the Holy Spirit?

CHAPTER SIX

Ben
"Rubberband Man"

As I stated earlier, I had asked the Lord to bring the people into my life that would help me heal. I asked for a clear sign—I received the first clear sign in an unexpected way. On March 21, 2005, a horrible tragedy took place at Red Lake, Minnesota. A high school student shot and killed 9 individuals and then turned the gun on himself. Since I worked at a public television station that had a local news program, we were inundated with phone calls and requests for video footage as well as interviews. It was a very stressful day. The next day, March 22nd, my stress level was so high by 5:00 that I had to go to the gym. As I was half way through my workout, I ran into someone that I had gotten to know at the Rec Center. His name is Ben. I had initially met Ben when he was my daughter's swimming instructor. My daughter absolutely loved having him as a swim teacher. We loved the fact that she enjoyed swimming lessons and that she could relate to Ben as a teacher. Ben is definitely the shy, quiet type of person. Ben is an incredible observer and takes things in all around him. Ben is also one of the best listeners I think I've met in my life. In my opinion, this is his greatest gift to the world. I think of Ben as being someone who would be more impressed by a job well done than something well said. I remember that Ben once told me that he didn't feel like he was contributing that much to this experience and I told him, "Ben, you are the gift." I also knew that Ben was a man of faith. We had shared a couple of discussions on faith and I had seen him at church a few times. I knew this was an important part of his life. So, as Ben was walking by me that evening in the Rec Center and asked me how I was doing, I really had to stop and think for a minute. It was a normal question but my answer wasn't. I said, "not very good" without even thinking about it. He stopped in his tracks, turned around and while looking me right in the eye he said, "what's wrong?" At that exact moment, I saw the face of Jesus Christ on Ben. A lot of people have asked me if I saw the actual face of Jesus Christ or if I saw Christ working in Ben. To this day, I tell people—"I saw the face of Jesus Christ." I knew that it was my sign. This was someone who was supposed to be in my life and was also supposed to be helping me in this journey. I can tell you now that seeing the vision of Christ on Ben's face is probably one of the most memorable moments in this entire journey. It is also a reminder to me that Christ works through people and when we are totally open to doing His will and letting Him work through us, others will see Christ in us. Seeing Christ in others may not always be a physical sign, but that persons' actions may be symbolic of Christ. Ben and I talked until he had to get ready for work but he made it clear that he was available to talk more if need be. Little did Ben know that this invitation would continue to lead us down a path of long friendship, many prayer sessions and a relationship that would serve as my stability through many of the challenging times that were in the future.

Two days later, I was shooting hoops and Ben walked over to check in and see how I was doing. I was floored. First of all, Ben is probably one of shiest guys I've ever met and secondly, I really didn't know him that well. The fact that he came over to check on me was once again a sign that he needed to be on my team. That same evening was Holy Thursday Mass and Father Mike Patnode did one of the most beautiful homilies I have ever heard about how each of us is the body of Christ and that each day of our lives we should be giving up ourselves for each other in service to do God's work. I reflected at the actions Ben had taken that week and how he had let himself be the body of Christ for me. He had put everything else aside to do God's work. I wrote Ben a letter of gratitude and gave it to him that Easter weekend. It was the start of a wonderful friendship and a new step for the team.

As the friendship with Ben developed and I had built up enough trust with him, I decided that it was time to tell him about the rape. It wasn't just that I needed to talk about it with the right person but that I really wanted him to understand why I was the way I was and why I would sometimes respond the way I did. I knew that having this basic background would help him help me. Sitting down and telling him was one of the hardest things I had done up to that point. Ben sat patiently and listened as I struggled to get the words out and to try and explain its impact on my life. I didn't cry like I thought I would and while I remember feeling relieved, I also remember feeling very vulnerable. Ben didn't say much at all. I kept thinking to myself-"what is he thinking?' That was very difficult for me. I wanted to know if it changed his opinion of me or if it didn't change anything at all. I needed to know that he would still accept me for who I was as a person and that it didn't matter. The more I thought about it, I realized that if anything, he probably had more respect for the things I was doing and he had a different appreciation for some of the challenges that I had probably been through to get to the point that I was at. For some reason, I think I was expecting him and others to think differently of me in a negative way. What I have learned, is that people don't react negatively at all. In fact, it is just the opposite. There is an incredible amount of respect and compassion as well as a recognition of the amount of strength and courage it has taken to even talk about the rape. As we left our meeting place, I asked Ben for a hug. For some reason, this was important to me. I think it was the needing to know that he wouldn't walk away or not be willing to support me in my efforts. He gave me a quick hug and we left. I felt strange that evening. I felt good about sharing the incident but I also knew that there was no turning back. I also knew that Ben would probably be the one person with whom I could share everything. At that point, I didn't realize the extent that this would be and how much that initial conversation would set the stage for an incredible prayer relationship. What I also didn't realize at the time was that it was the first time I was really able to trust a man, other than my husband, again.

   The next day, I saw Ben at the gym. Unfortunately, he had just sprained his ankle. I was sitting with him while he was icing his ankle and I asked him how he felt about what I had shared with him. He said it was a bit of a "shocker" but he was o.k. about knowing and here to support me in any way that he could. He asked if I had been up all night over analyzing everything I had shared with him the previous night. I told him that I had actually slept well and was relieved that he knew. I told him that if he ever had any questions that I would be happy to answer them. My feeling was that since he was willing to be there for me, I needed to open myself up to fill in any information that he needed as well. This was the last time that we talked about it for a while. I offered to soak and massage Ben's feet for him to help with the swelling. I told him that I would come over that evening. I soaked and massaged Ben's feet and I hoped that it gave him some relief for at least a little while. I didn't think about it until later, but someone pointed out to me that Ben was the person in whom I had seen Christ. In the Bible, the washing of the feet was a key part of the Last Supper. How ironic it was that I was washing and massaging the feet of the man in whom I had seen Christ. Knowing what I do now, I don't think it was a coincidence that I was at the gym when Ben sprained his ankle or that he was willing to let me soak and massage his feet.

After he had washed their feet, he put his cloak back on and reclined at table once more. He said to them: "Do you understand what I just did for you? You address me as 'Teacher' and "Lord,' and fittingly enough, for that is what I am. But if I washed your

feet—I who am Teacher and Lord—then you must wash each other's feet. What I just did was to give you an example: as I have done, so you must do. I solemnly assure you, no slave is greater than his master; no messenger outranks the one who sent him. Once you know all these things, blest will you be if you put them into practice.
John 13:12-17

Ben and Deb after a team dinner.

A Look Into the Future As it Relates to This:

An interesting event happened in the days before Holy Thursday, April 13th, 2006. A few weeks before that date, I received a call from Tammy at the church office asking me if I would be willing to have my feet washed by Father Vincent on Holy Thursday. I immediately felt the Holy Spirit energy running through my body. I told Tammy that this was an amazing phone call for two reasons. The first reason was that I had written the part about washing Ben's feet just weeks before the phone call and secondly, I felt it was God's way of sending a message to me in terms of my journey at this point. The washing of the feet was scheduled for April 13th. Throughout the day, I found myself preparing mentally for what I knew would be taking place that evening. I knew this was something very special and that it would have a profound impact on me. John (another team member) told me that he wanted to go to Mass with me as long as it wouldn't affect the experience that I wanted as a part of the Holy Thursday Mass. I told him that I would welcome the opportunity to share this mass with him.

Just prior to the start of the feet washing part, I felt an incredible sense of peace, energy and joy all mixed together. As I looked to the top of the church, I had a sense of the Holy Spirit filling the entire top of the ceiling. It was both a sight and sensing thing. As my feet were washed, I felt God's grace move through my entire body. I let my heart take it in and continue growing. I didn't cry like I thought I would but rather, I felt an amazing WOW inside. As Father Vincent got done, he kissed my feet and gave me the most incredible look. I felt complete, I felt fulfillment. I felt Christ. As I got back to my pew, I looked up and Christ was there, in the midst of the Holy Spirit on the ceiling. That's when I felt the tears. Throughout the entire Eucharist, I felt His presence like I had never felt before. I kept thinking that I might pass out from all the energy. It was almost a surreal experience. I remember noting how much Father Vincent's hands were shaking during the blessing of the bread and wine. I don't recall seeing him shake like this at any other time.

My friend John and I talked after Mass and he told me that I gave him this smile right before it started and said, honestly, I looked 20 years younger. He also said that he felt this incredible Holy Spirit energy throughout this experience. He said he almost felt like he was experiencing it through me and with me at the same time. We drove around afterwards to talk about this because it was so profound for both of us.

I was once again in awe of His grace and mercy. I also wished that I had set up a time to wash the feet of each of the team members. I wanted to pass on the humbleness that I had seen in Father Vincent to each of the team members. I told John that at some point, I really want to wash the feet of all of our team members. It became something very important to me. I hope that there is an opportunity to do this at some point in the future.

CHAPTER SEVEN

Jamie K
"Bad Monkey"

Every once in awhile, you meet someone in your life who just makes you smile. Jamie is one of those types of people. I had still been continuing to pray for God to bring the right people into my life. Jamie wasn't as obvious as Ben and P.J. had been, but she has become just as much a part of the team as anyone else. I really started getting to know her when she was working the morning shift at the Rec Center. Every time I came in, she always greeted me with a big smile. She also always had a kind word to say. One morning, however, when I went to workout, Jamie did not look like she normally does. I really had the feeling that something was wrong. I asked her how she was and at first she was hesitant about saying something but as she looked into my eyes, she couldn't hold it back anymore. She broke down and started crying and proceeded to tell me about a breakup with her boyfriend. She was really having a difficult time. I sat and listened for a while until she felt better. I kept checking in with her throughout the week. I knew it was such a difficult time for her. The interesting thing was that through helping her with her pain, I knew that she was meant to be the next person added to the team. Anyone who could open up to me without knowing me that well would be capable of helping me in my healing process. I made a point of getting to know Jamie better and I continued to pray for the wisdom to know when I should talk with her about the incident. That time came in July. Jamie had come over to our house for dinner one night and we were just sitting and chatting after dinner. Something told me that it was the right time to tell her. I let her know that I had something important to share with her. She listened very closely and we both shared some tears. I didn't tell her all the details as it was difficult enough to tell her the first part. I told her that at some point she may need to hear it but for now, I just needed her to know that it happened and how it contributed to the person I was today. She told me that it really helped her to know about the incident because it filled in pieces of a puzzle for her. My weight issue now took on a different meaning and she felt it could help her to help me. I haven't talked much about the weight issue but this is a good place to explain it in more detail. One of the things that I struggled with, especially after the rape, was my appearance. What I thought at the time was that if I weren't as attractive, I wouldn't be a potential rape victim. Therefore, if I could hide behind extra weight, I would remain "safe" and "protected" from being raped. Of course, I know now that this isn't the case at all with rape. Rape is about control and violence, it isn't about how attractive someone is or isn't. Unfortunately, I didn't know that at the time and rather than dealing with the rape as I should have, I used every other coping mechanism available, including gaining a lot of extra weight. After sharing all of this information with Jamie, our relationship became even stronger. Words and actions took on different meanings.

One interesting fact about Jamie is that while Ben, P.J. and John are all Catholic, Jamie is not. This isn't to say that she doesn't believe in God, but she practiced her faith in another way. In one intensive prayer session that Ben and I did in December, I received a very clear indication that God would like me to assist Him in a healing for Jamie. Jamie has very serious back problems. She was facing possible back surgery in the summer of 2006 and this was obviously weighing very heavy on her mind. At this point in the process, I didn't know a lot about healing sessions. I had ordered a couple of books that Lisa had suggested because she really felt that God was giving me the gift of healing. I had devoured the books but still didn't know a lot about how to do a healing session. I continued to pray for God's guidance in how to bring about his healing. His messages were very clear. The first step was that she needed a total conversion to Him and a total surrender of faith and trust in Him. The second step was that she needed to believe 100% in her heart that a healing was possible. I knew that the first step was definitely going to be easier than the second step. Jamie knew how severe her back situation was and several times she told me that she just didn't see how it was possible. Many times, I referenced scripture of God's healing.

The first opportunity for deep prayer with Jamie presented itself spontaneously. Jamie had stopped by my office at work. We were talking about school, her schedule and any other basic topics. As Jamie started talking about several things, I could tell she was very emotional and obviously hurting about a few things. She talked and I listened. All of a sudden, I heard God telling me that she and I needed to pray. There were some things that she needed to hear. We joined hands and I invited Jesus Christ and the Holy Spirit into our discussion. I asked the Lord to fill us with the words that needed to be said. I don't even remember everything that was said, but I know it was powerful. Both Jamie and I had tears flowing down our cheeks almost the entire time. Our hands were shaking so intensely with the power of the Holy Spirit that it was running up and down my arms. When the words stopped flowing, both Jamie and I remained frozen. The incredible sensation of peace, love and the Holy Spirit was awesome. I would have loved to remain in that moment for a very long time. This prayer session impacted me as much as it did Jamie. I was once again reminded of just how incredibly powerful prayer can be!

Jamie's spiritual healing continued one night when Ben and Jamie had come over for dinner. We had a lovely dinner of fondue to celebrate the New Year. After dinner and the kids had gone to bed, we got into a very deep discussion about Medjagorje and how one book on the topic had impacted me. Medjagorje refers to a village in western Yugoslavia where since June 24, 1981, hundreds of apparitions of the Virgin

Mary have occurred. You will find more information about Medjagorje in Chapter Ten. As we continued the discussion, Jamie began to start talking about her faith, where she was at and where she needed to be. After a certain point in the discussion, I asked her if she wanted to pray and she did, so, Ben, Jamie and I sat in a circle on my living room floor and prayed together. It was an amazing experience. It was the first time that our group had prayed together in that way. The presence of God and the Holy Spirit was so strong. I knew that we had started Jamie on the path for spiritual healing and once we could accomplish that, we could begin to focus on her physical healing.

Jamie's Corner:

Every so often when you allow your true colors to show, you will run across an individual who will have a profound effect on your life. These individuals are few and far between. When you find someone like this, not only cherish them but hold them dear to your heart. I consider myself blessed having four such individuals in my life.

When I first met Deb working at the recreation center, I had no idea she would be the individual who would give me inspiration and strength like never before. Every morning, she would come in to work out with a radiant gleam to her smile and something pleasant to say. We never engaged in deep conversation but the first time we did is forever burned in my memory.

Like any other morning, Deb walked into the recreation center with her radiant smile and the ambition to workout. As she approached the desk, that radiant smile and ambition turned to a look of concern staring back at me. I knew I was in trouble when I saw that because I knew she could read me. There she stood at the desk with her card in hand as time froze in place for an instant. Deb proceeded to say, "you don't look so good. Are you o.k.?" Right then and there, I lost it. I couldn't control the tears no matter how hard I tried because my heart hurt and for the first time, I couldn't hide or handle it.

For over two hours, Deb stood there and listened to my story of love, hurt and heartache. She didn't say much. She didn't have to because it was all said through her eyes when I found the strength to lift my head and look at her through my blurred teary vision. To this day, that love, hurt and heartache still exists within me. Yes, the tears still flow, but that strength and inspiration Deb bestowed on me that morning still thrives within my heart and soul. That morning, merely an acquaintance became so much more.

At one point in my life, I was spiritual and found comfort in the stars as I reflected back upon the day. As I got more involved with the church, I drifted away from my spiritual side because all it came down to was money. This put a sour taste in my mouth because religion isn't supposed to be all about money. It's about being there for each other, serving your God, and keeping the faith alive within and around you.

When I first came to BSU, I was excited, driven, sociable, studious and not focused on religion. I knew that somewhere there was a plan for me and all I had to do was figure that plan out. Once I figured that big plan out, I would be golden. Yes, I could do that on my own... So, the first thing I tried figuring out is where I would be in ten years with my big plan. If I could unlock my future, I would be able to live in the present "correctly". This would include taking the right classes for my future career, having the jobs that would look great on a resume and making connections with individuals who could help me along the way. This isn't going to be so bad.

After a couple of semesters trying to figure out who I was going to be in ten years, I found myself incredibly stressed out. I couldn't focus, I couldn't study anymore, my grades slipped, my boyfriend and I broke up, friends tried committing suicide, my family wasn't doing the best and there I sat by myself lost in the midst of it all. Luckily, I had a few close friends who helped me through and motivated me to keep trying. Playing intramural sports, working out and learning the art and grace of ballroom, latin and swing dancing also helped me relieve this stress for the time being.

This stress went on for another year of school. I avoided dealing with it by keeping myself constantly busy. I had four jobs, school, intramural athletics, student programming meetings and swing dance club. I would sleep whenever I had time. This worked pretty well, but I wasn't moving forward because I wasn't dealing with the stress of my big plan. This is when I met Deb.

I finally realized that no one knows where he or she is going to be in ten years or even next week for that matter. I had just spent the last two years so focused on figuring out my future and trying to plan for it that I forgot to live in the present. I was lost in the background of life just observing it instead of living it. Knowing that no one in bodily form could tell me my big plan in life, I had to get back to my faith and trust in God believing there is a plan for me.

Deb was the beginning of my reconnection with God and my spiritual side. With that, I'd like to share a couple specific instances of powerful prayer.

Before last year, I'd never prayed with someone. Prayer is very personal, very intimate and with my guard up, I wasn't going to let anyone in to see that side of me because I didn't want to risk getting hurt. I had the "I look out for me" mentality "because no one else will". One day, I was walking through campus and something told me to stop in and say hello to Deb. It was a good day with no more classes or work to follow. I went to see Deb because she always makes the day even better! It was toward the end of fall semester and everything was piling on so it was nice to escape for a while. Deb and I caught up on things that were going on in our lives and eventually it led to how school was going for me thus far and what classes I was going to take next semester. I hadn't even really thought about which classes I was going to take next semester and I was instantly overwhelmed. All of a sudden, that stress of my big plan in life and determining my future came pouring into my body. I could literally feel it. My mind started racing, my heart pounded. I felt this heat serge go through my body from head to toe and my hands shook slightly. I swore my heart was going to burst within me. There was no escaping this and I had to get it out. With a few moments of shock, I broke down and told Deb how difficult it was to plan for the future because of the unknown. At this point of my life, there was so much pressure to figure out what I wanted to do with my life, more so my career and I just didn't know. I felt as though I was blindfolded being pushed down some path not knowing if it was straight, going in a circle or whether it was right or wrong. The one thing I did know was that I was stumbling on this path and felt as though I may collapse from the fatigue. I like to see where I'm going so I can plan for it but not being able to see my path upset me to the point of thinking God was doing this on purpose. I was upset with God for hiding my plan from me. I trusted Him but that faltered at times because I couldn't stand to fall. What it boiled down to was that I didn't want to fall in front of God, my family or my friends because everyone saw me as a strong individual. With that reputation, I felt as though I had to be invincible and strong for everyone around me. What I didn't know was that by setting aside my stress and my problems to help others be strong, I would become weak. It felt good helping others and that would temporarily mend my unspoken problems but it never took them away. My heart could only take so much and that day in Deb's office, it couldn't take anymore.

At this point, Deb took my hands and asked if we could pray together. I agreed because that's exactly what I felt was needed. We closed our eyes and she began to pray aloud. We were connected not only through the hands but also through our hearts. I could feel it in my heart and it blew me away because I never knew something so powerful existed. The whole time, I couldn't stop the tears from rolling down my face because for the first time in my life, I truly felt the presence of God within my heart. It was at this time that both Deb's and my hands began to shake with this incredible energy flow between us, God and the Spirit. When we were finished praying, Deb and I sat there still feeling the energy and present of God all around us. We were immobilized and couldn't find ourselves so that we could move. I felt His message and His love for me. It was so overwhelming because I couldn't understand why He loved and cared about me unconditionally. It just blew my mind. Never before had I felt inner peace like that. I was in a state of "being" and I was content. God sent a powerful message through Deb and it is forever in my heart. Just reflecting on this moment has brought years and that peace back to me once again. Deb showed me the power of prayer in number and it was the experience of a lifetime.

The Prayer Trio

Not all of the individuals on the team personally know each other. We were all connected through Deb and therefore trusted each other because we know what type of person Deb opens herself to. Since she opened her heart to all of us, we knew there existed similar values among us which allowed for trust and strength. Each of us bring a different aspect to the team which has made this team strong and complete. To strengthen our sense of team, Deb and her family would invite us over for dinner to be a part of the family and to connect. Since both Ben and myself had to stay in Bemidji over the '05-'06 New Year, Deb and her family invited us over to have dinner early in January. I knew Ben through work and teaching swimming lessons at the recreation center, but I didn't really know him. I viewed him as quiet and mysterious as well as very trustworthy, strong-minded, determined, and religious. To tell the truth, I still don't know him well, but that's the beauty of this team because it works.

The dinner was amazing as was the conversation. Once the dishes were done, Ben, Deb and myself sat in the Living Room and talked since we hadn't connected with each other for so long due to the business of the season. The conversation soon led to thoughts of religion. Ben and Deb go to the same

Catholic Church every Sunday and know a lot about their faith and are very comfortable in it. For some reason, I felt uncomfortable talking with them about faith and religion because I'm still working on figuring that out for myself. I was raised Lutheran and couldn't talk about religion and faith because all of my close friends were strong Catholics who would tell me I'm going to hell for being Lutheran. For some reason, this conversation with Deb and Ben both being Catholic triggered that memory and I didn't want to talk about religion because I'd be shot down. I knew this wasn't the case but it was in the back of my mind.

Before I knew it, they were asking me about my thoughts on religion. I was instantly overwhelmed with questions. My heart started pounding and I felt the heat move through my body from head to toe. I was choked up and just broke down. I felt inferior in this conversation and didn't care for it. If I recall correctly, I believe what triggered this reaction was talking about faith and the effects on families. At this time, my family wasn't doing so well and I was especially worried about my younger sister. I started talking to Ben and Deb about my family situation and just lost it. Deb had this strong sense that we needed to pray. There we sat, all three of us cross-legged on the living room carpet holding hands and closing our eyes. Deb began to pray aloud and I felt my heart open. I felt a connection with Ben, Deb, God and the Spirit. As the prayer continued, our hands began shaking and God's grace came pouring in. It wasn't as intense as when it was just Deb and myself in her office, but to share that with the three of us really meant a lot. I don't like people seeing me like that, so it was a huge step for me to let Ben see me in shambles. After Deb was done praying aloud, Ben and I silently said our prayers and when it was finished, we all knew. The peace among us was the only thing left. For the first time, a part of our team connected like never before. I'm very grateful for that experience. I've never connected like that with Ben before and don't know if I ever will because the times are changing. If anything else, I'd like to say, "thank you, Ben, for showing me a side of yourself I've never seen before. I truly feel honored."

You Are
Dedicated to Deb
By Jamie Kaehler

Truthfully; you are a
Rare individual who
Enchants the lives of many.
Angelic in a sense
Shown through your
Unconditional love in the
Realms off the universe.
Endeared by those who surround you;
Deeply inspired and moved are those who love you...

For I know well the plans I have in mind for you, says the Lord, plans for your welfare, not for woe! Plans to give you a future full of hope. When you call me, when you go to pray to me, I will listen to you. When you look for me, you will find me. Yes, when you seek me with all your heart, you will find me with you, says the Lord, and I will change your lot; I will gather you together from all the nations and all the places to which I have banished you, says the Lord, and bring you back to the place from which I have exiled you.
Jeremiah 29: 11-15

"Again I tell you, if two of you join your voices on earth to pray for anything whatever, it shall be granted

you by my Father in heaven. Where two or three are gathered in my name, there am I in their midst."
Matthew 18: 19-20

Later, on the occasion of a Jewish feast, Jesus went up to Jerusalem. Now in Jerusalem by the Sheep Pool there is a place with the Hebrew name Bethesda. Its five porticoes were crowded with sick people lying there blind, lame or disabled. There was one man who had been sick for thirty-eight years. Jesus, who knew he had been sick a long time, said when he saw him lying there, "Do you want to be healed?" "Sir," the sick man answered, "I do not have anyone to plunge me into the pool once the water has been stirred up. By the time I get there, someone else has gone in ahead of me. Jesus said to him, "Stand up! Pick up your mat and walk!" The man was immediately cured; he picked up his mat and began to walk.
John 5: 1-9

Points to Ponder:

Have you ever prayed with someone else? Find someone or a group that you trust and pray with them. You will be amazed at the power of prayer in numbers.

How strong is your faith? Do you believe that God can heal someone here on Earth?

A Prayer to St. Peregrine for Sick Relatives and Friends

O great St. Peregrine, you have been called "The Mighty", "The Wonder Worker" because of the numerous miracles which you obtained from God for those who have turned to you in their need. For so many years, you bore in your own flesh this cancerous disease that destroys the very fiber of our being.

You turned to God when the power of human beings could do no more, and you were favored with the vision of Jesus coming down from His cross to heal your affliction. I now ask God to heal these sick persons whom I entrust to you:

(mention their names here)

Aided by your powerful intercession, I shall sing with Mary a hymn of gratitude to God for His great goodness and mercy. Amen.

Jamie K & Deb after a team dinner.

CHAPTER EIGHT

The Existence of Satan

Whoever believes that satan doesn't exist needs to read this chapter. I had faithfully been praying and working through my *Miracle Hour* book. As I continued to do this, more and more of my past continued to surface. I continued to try and work through all of these things on my own, but at some point, I realized that I needed to talk with someone else about it. I already knew in my heart that the person needed to be Ben. I saw Ben at the pool on Monday and told him that I would appreciate some time from him when he had it. I probably should have been a little more "forceful" in my request because the following week turned out to be one of the worst in my life. In fact, knowing what I do now, I realize that I was under a major satanic attack. I should have recognized it, but like every human being, there are times that satan, with his cunning ways, will get into our lives and it isn't until divine intervention that we see it for what it is. One thing I have learned is that the closer a person is to doing God's work or the closer someone is to doing something "big" for the Lord, satan will try and interfere. I started getting very depressed. I was also ridden with anxiety and I couldn't sleep. I was consumed by nightmares about the rape and so many things surrounding it. I couldn't talk with my husband about it because I just didn't want him to know how horrible it had been. Instead, I paced the halls, I cried in the living room chair and I literally started driving myself into a state of severe depression. I didn't want my husband to touch me at all. It was as if I needed his support the most at this time but I couldn't take it. My sister was also visiting for a week. She knew something was wrong but didn't know what. She and Stephen were preparing to leave for Montana with our kids. I didn't know if I was happy or terrified that they were leaving. I was at a point where I didn't know if I wanted to live anymore. I didn't care and I wasn't afraid to die. I was in an incredible fog and big state of confusion. As they drove down the driveway, I remember thinking that I really wondered if I would see them again, or if I had said my final goodbye. I had also stopped praying during this week. It was as if something had a horrible hold on me. The only way I can accurately describe it is like I was under a cloud of darkness--pure darkness. I knew I wasn't myself but I couldn't seem to drag myself up. I actually started thinking about the ways that I could kill myself without bringing harm to anyone else. I started organizing everything at work so that my projects wouldn't get lost. I was making lists of everything with deadlines so someone could pick up easily. On the home front, I made sure the bills were paid. I started writing letters to my family and friends. Even as I write this, I can't believe that I did these things. When I say this to you now, it's like that wasn't even me. This can tell you how powerful satan is. He was able to penetrate into me because I wasn't careful and I wasn't praying like I needed to be. He is cunning and he is evil. But more importantly, God

IS MORE POWERFUL! We just have to make sure we are relying on Him and continuing to do the right things for Him. On Thursday of the same week, I had to bring something over to P.J. He took one look at me and knew that something was seriously wrong. He told me later that I looked absolutely exhausted and depressed. He told me to sit down and start talking. All I could do was start crying. We talked for as much time as he had but he got me to commit to going to the gym the next morning. I think he knew that I'd see Ben and I think he also knew that Ben was the person who was going to be able to help me get out of this hole.

Unbeknownst to me, Jamie had also been clued in to the fact that something was wrong. She and I had exchanged a couple of e-mails and she knew that something was wrong but was leaving for Canada and knew there wouldn't be time to really work through it prior to her leaving. She did talk with Ben and gave him a heads up that something was wrong. On Friday morning, when I entered the Rec Center, the look on Ben's face said it all. He asked me how I was and tried to get me to start talking. I told him that I just couldn't talk about this right now or in this location. I told him that I wanted to work out first and then maybe we would be able to talk. About half way through the work out, I got a basketball and I told him that I was exhausted and depressed and that yes, I did need to talk. Unfortunately, he was leaving town for the weekend, but we agreed that we would connect on Monday so that I could talk and process with him. It was a very long weekend. I was fine until Friday afternoon and the dark thoughts started coming again. I started drinking and in all honestly, spent much of the weekend under the influence of alcohol. It was the only way I could deal with the amount of pain that I had brought to the surface that needed to be dealt with. By Sunday morning, I was a wreck and again in the suicidal mode. I remember getting down on my knees and asking God for a miracle. What I heard back was clean and to the point, "I've put the people in your life to help you.. Use them!" At the same time, images of Ben, Jamie and P.J. were shown to me. Once again, it was God's way of reinforcing to me that these people had been sent to me for a reason and that God did have a special plan for them as it related to me. It was time to ask for help. It was time to take the next step. I was not in control anymore. God was in charge and He was leading me to where I needed to be.

I made it to work on Monday morning but I was not in good shape. I was going through the motions and was hoping that Ben and I would have time to talk so that I could begin working through the black hole. We were finally able to connect at the Rec Center pool while he was doing his life guarding shift. I honestly don't know if he was more relieved to see me or if I was more relieved to see him. I asked him when we could talk and he thought we should talk right then. I told him that I didn't think I could talk with him about these things at the pool. He tried to convince me otherwise. For the first few minutes, I didn't know what to do. I almost got up and left. I didn't know where to start and I was afraid of breaking down at the pool. Ben sat patiently and looked at me with the most open, caring expression. I knew God had put him there. I knew I needed to talk. I took a deep breath and started talking. I told Ben about the nightmares. I told him some of the details about the rape and how these details were starting to bother me and consume my thoughts. I told him about my fears, my insecurities and I finally told him how depressed I was and that I had been suicidal. This was probably the most difficult thing to tell him. Telling him about the rape was hard, but telling him about the suicide was even harder. The rape was something that someone else had done to me but the suicide would have been a choice that I made. Knowing how much that I respect life and God's plans for us, the suicide component is so hard to comprehend. I know that it was hard for Ben to hear about this. I know it was hard to listen to all of this information but he did it and once again, my gratitude for him was so strong. I talked until the end of his pool shift and I felt so much better. I remember feeling as if an incredible weight had been lifted off my shoulders. As we were walking out, Ben told me that it made him feel good to know that he could help me. It made him feel good to be needed and know that his help could make such a difference. He told me that it was an honor and privilege to help me. He gave me a big hug and I told him over and over how much I appreciated him. I can honestly say that I was afraid to let go of that hug at that moment. I knew that I had a lot more to deal with and in that hug, I felt safe. I felt comforted, accepted and at peace. We decided to meet the next morning for a bike ride around the lake. I made Ben promise not to laugh at me knowing I would be twice as slow as him. I also told him that I would probably have to stop and take a break a few times. Ben told me not to worry about it and he seemed excited about doing the bike ride. I found myself smiling and looking forward to the ride. It was such a great feeling to smile after the previous week that had been filled with so much depression.

The next morning, Ben and I biked around the lake. I learned that I was definitely much slower than Ben but that he wasn't concerned about that at all. We had a wonderful time and finished up our conversation from the previous day. We also had a chance to talk about Ben a little too. I learned more about him and it made me feel more comfortable after getting to know some things about him. I also asked him if he would pray with me the following week. He told me that he would be willing to do that. I was relieved, because I knew that needed to be the next step in my process. I also knew that I needed to complete a trip to California in the meantime, so I had to get focused on that. Another great thing happened that day, which was that I had the opportunity to meet Ben's parents. I was immediately at ease with them. They are very nice people and it was so good to meet the individuals that gave life to Ben. I remember thanking them for the gift of Ben and I also remember telling them what an awesome man Ben was and how lucky I was that he was in my life. I told them that I was grateful for his presence in both mine and my families' life. I'm sure at the time, they were thinking—what is going on here? How is it that Ben has gotten to know Deb so well and what is the nature of their relationship? I told them that Ben was a part of "my team" and that he had helped me tremendously with my workout plan and support. I don't think I would have been able to explain the magnitude of all of the different types of support. I figured that there may be a time and place to discuss the nature of this relationship but I also knew it would be a long time from this initial meeting. For the time being, it was great just to enjoy their company and the wonderful conversation.

I left for my trip in California and realized quickly that I was still very depressed. In fact, I started making another list of things that I needed to talk to Ben about. By Sunday, I finally decided to call him. I didn't reach him in the afternoon and left a message. I tried back on Sunday night and he answered the phone.

I was trying to make a conversation and realized that he didn't want to be having a conversation. I was confused. He told me that if I needed to talk, he would listen and yet I needed to talk and he wanted to get off the phone. I was frustrated, depressed and a little angry. I didn't want to push, so I told him that I would talk to him in Bemidji. I think he knew I was a little upset but I don't think he knew what to do. After returning to Bemidji, I saw him on Tuesday at the Rec. He asked me if I was coming in to talk with him at the pool. I told him that I didn't think so. He asked if I was sure. I said—yes. I have no idea if he realized how upset I had been. I knew that I needed to go and talk with him but I was angry and didn't know if I could effectively talk with him anyway. I also knew that I needed to pray with him. I decided to get P.J.'s opinion on what I should do. His feeling was that I should go talk with him at the pool. If it felt right, I should go ahead and try and pray with him later that evening, as scheduled. If it didn't feel right, I could just let it go. I realized that P.J. was probably right. I went to the pool and met Ben. I think he was surprised that I showed up based on our conversation earlier in the day. I started by telling him how upset I had been about the phone conversation. He explained his perception of the call that evening. I also told him that I really needed to pray with him so I could move this process forward. We agreed to meet that evening at my house. I don't know if I was more nervous or excited but I definitely knew that it was what needed to be done. That evening turned out to be one of the biggest turning points in this journey.

The strategies that satan uses:

In my experience, there are five major areas that satan uses in an attempt to deter us from keeping our focus on God and doing His work. If you understand this, you are armed with information. Scripture and prayer as well as this knowledge help you with your "armor"! The first area is discouragement (guilt/shame/unworthiness). In this area, we focus inward and don't put our trust in God. The second area is procrastination. Satan attempts to get us to not get things done and therefore makes it difficult to move forward. The third area is failure/defeat. Satan wants us to think that if we try, we may fail and therefore, we shouldn't even try. The fourth area is an attempt to throw us off course. He almost creates a delusion in which the wrong things look and feel right and then we will desire those things more than the correct things. A true test of this is God's word. Is what your doing in line with scripture? Finally, satan creates doubt and confusion. One of the biggest ways he does this is by keeping us feeling shame and guilt about our sins and really doubting whether or not we truly receive God's grace and forgiveness. Again, go to scripture. What does God tell us about grace and forgiveness? Why did Jesus die on the cross? Whenever I start feeling doubt, I command satan, in the name of Jesus, Christ, our Lord to leave. I then ask for our Lord to bring me His peace and understanding of what He wants for me. Praise the Lord for telling us in scripture what we need to do to beat the devil's schemes and tactics! I hope this information will help you stomp the devil and therefore be able to do even more of Our Lord's work!

Jamie's Corner:

The Black Box

Sometimes the simple little things of life allow me to sit back, smile and relax at the thought of being.

It gives me a sense of belonging in this magnificently huge world. There is nothing like feeling you are a part of something truly wonderful. As strange as this may seem, I sometimes relate life to a buoy that I observe every so often out on Lake Bemidji when times get rough. With that I'd like to share a little story with you about 'my buoy':

It floats on the surface of the water bobbing gently as the waves push up along side of it. There is tension on the buoy from the waves because it's resisting them. This small, round, white buoy is winning the "battle" against the strong, blue waves. I would have never thought that something so small could be so powerful.

This small, round, white buoy reminds me of the smaller details of this world, myself. Sometimes I feel as though I am fighting just to stay afloat at sea. The violent waves can push me around all they want, maybe even dent my outer shell, but they will never crack it. I somehow always find a way to stay afloat at sea because that is my will. Something keeps pushing me to strive for the best and reminding me to never give up faith. I can tell myself "hey, if a buoy can fight this sea, so can I."

What if I can't fight anymore and my buoy's shell completely cracks? There I sit completely drained of faith and soon thereafter life. I've been there. Life can be overwhelming to the point of pushing you over the edge making your mind play tricks on you instead of following your heart's intuition. There may come a point where your mind drowns out your heart completely and then life is lost on a healthy emotional level-maybe on a physical level as well.

In August of 2005, Deb secretly hit the point of losing her life on a healthy emotional level. She had an attack of the heart by her mind that lead to her mind playing tricks and deceiving her of options. Deb was in a trap and felt as though she had no way out. Luckily enough for both of us, I sensed that.

Over that summer, Deb and I had corresponded through emails virtually everyday even though I saw her virtually every morning for her workout. She didn't show up one morning. I thought nothing of it because sometimes she had meetings and couldn't make it in. So I just sent her an email before I got off my desk shift saying that I missed not seeing her smiling face walking through the door that morning. I went about my day with school and studying thinking nothing was wrong.

Right before I had gone to bed, I checked my email to see what Deb wrote back because she always checks her email and responds the same day. To my surprise, there wasn't a reply from her. I just told myself she didn't have time tonight due to a hectic schedule or something along those lines.

Then next morning at work, I didn't see Deb and hadn't heard from her. This threw up a red flag and I somehow knew something was very wrong because this was not characteristic of Deb. Again, I sent her an email asking if everything was all right because I had a sense of urgency in regards to her and I didn't know why. She didn't respond to my phone calls but two days later I finally got a reply through email saying that she had a lot of things on her mind but that she didn't want to talk about them. Deb thought that she would be distracting me from having a good time on my vacation that I was leaving for the next day.

Let's just say with an email reply like that I was freaking out! Something is wrong and she won't talk to me about it because she doesn't want to rain on my parade. This is not Deb talking. She had to get out whatever was holding her down because this was not healthy and I knew it.

Thursday night, my last night in Bemidji before I left for vacation, I made it a point to go visit Ben at work and tell him what was going on with Deb. I told him everything that I knew about the situation; Deb not coming to workout like usual, her avoidance of conversation with me and most definitely the disturbing email. I told Ben that he had to talk with her because my hands were tied being she totally shut me out.

That night, I drove down to the cities and flew out to Detroit early the next day where I would meet up with a couple of my Canadian friends from Ontario. I was excited but extremely nervous and uneasy about leaving because I knew something wasn't right with Deb. I could only pray that God would get her through this.

A couple nights into my vacation, I received a phone call from Deb crying over the line. The first thing she said to me was, "You saved my life Jamie." I was speechless because my mind was racing but no words would come out. She went on to tell me about how she had sat down and began writing letters to her husband, Steve, and her two children, Madeleine and Ryan. She had planned on committing suicide that night-that is until she ran into Ben at the recreation center. Deb told me that Ben had asked her if she was all right and she had replied that she was but he didn't believe her. Ben then told her that he had talked to me and that I was very concerned with her well-being. Right then, she knew she was 'in trouble' and we as a team weren't going to let it go unnoticed. She had told me that if I hadn't picked up on it that she doesn't know if she would be here today. There's an overwhelmingly great feeling; "I saved a life...I saved Deb's life..."

More so though, we as a team came through to lift Deb's spirits in order to not only come back to her heart's intuition but also to regain her life of faith. We as a team stood strong and through that experience became closer. I believe this to be the first time our team truly felt united being we all played a role in saving Deb's life. I love you Deb and I don't know what I'd do without you smiling my worries away. Thank you for staying with us.

If you are angry, let it be without sin. The sun must not go down on your wrath; do not give the devil a chance to work on you.
Ephesians 4:26-27

The thief comes only to steal and slaughter and destroy. I came that they might have life and have it to the full.
John 10:10

The devil then took him up a very high mountain and displayed before him all the kingdoms off the world in their magnificence, promising, "All these will I bestow on you if you prostrate yourself in homage before me." To this, Jesus said to him, "Away with you, Satan! Scripture has it: 'You shall do homage to the Lord your God; him alone shall you adore.'" At that the devil left him, and angels came and waited on him.
Matthew 4: 8-11

Do not be conquered by evil but conquer evil with good.
Romans 12:21

Prayers to St. Michael the Archangel:

Saint Michael, the Archangel, defend us in battle; be our protection against the wickedness and snares of the devil. May God rebuke him, we humbly pray; and do thou, O Prince of the Heavenly Host, by the power of God, thrust into Hell Satan and the other evil spirits who prowl about the world seeking the ruin of souls. Amen.

Prince of the heavenly hosts, conqueror of the infernal dragon, you received from God the strength and power to destroy through humility the pride of the powers of darkness. We implore you help us to true humility of heart, to unshakable fidelity, to fulfill the Will of God and to fortitude in sufferings and trials. Help us to stand before the judgment seat of God. Amen.

Points to Ponder:

What are some ways that satan is making his presence known in your life right now? How is he trying to hold you hostage from the grace and mercy of God?

Pray for the Lord to take away the evil ways of Satan so that you can open your heart to God's work and fill your heart with the love and abundance of God's grace and mercy.

CHAPTER NINE

Forgiving Others

Ben arrived at my home in the early evening of August 16th to help me begin the process of forgiving the men who had raped me as well as the individuals who stood by and watched without calling for help. To say I was a little nervous would be an understatement. I think Ben was probably a little nervous too although I know he wanted to be strong for both of us. We began by completing prayers of surrender and spiritual warfare. I then completed the prayers of the Holy Spirit and asked for the return of memories so that I could complete healing and the process of praying for forgiveness. Ben and I went from the very beginning until the end, recalling each and every detail that the Holy Spirit presented to us. When memories were presented, I asked the Lord to forgive the person(s) for the act(s) and I also asked for God's presence to come into each individual's life. I turned over every act and emotion for healing. With each passing act of forgiveness, I continued to feel my shoulders lighten and my body began to experience peace. I knew that in my heart, I was really forgiving these individuals. I also knew that through this forgiveness, I would lose so much of the anger, resentment, frustration and feelings of helplessness about the situation. I don't know if I have ever cried so hard or felt so much pain as when I went through the process. The interesting thing is that as I felt those emotions, I also felt so much freedom—I was finally ready to move forward and really heal from this experience. Ben was very supportive, calm, focused and compassionate. He was the rock that I needed to make it through this process.

The next morning when I woke up, I was very emotionally tired but I also felt good. I felt a peace that I had not experienced for so long. I went outside and took a walk. It had been ages since I had gone for a walk outside and felt the type of peace that I was feeling. I kept smiling at everything. I smiled at the road. I smiled at the bridge. I kept gazing to the sky and thanking God. I was back and it felt so good. Later that day, I saw Ben and he immediately checked in to see how I was doing. He could tell from the smile on my face that I was definitely much better than I had been the night before. I think he was pretty surprised at the big change in me from the previous evening. For the first time in a long time, I looked in the mirror and saw that I was a beautiful person. Praise the Lord!

Ben's Corner:

The thing that stands out the most in my mind about the night Deb asked forgiveness of those who raped her was Deb's physical appearance the day after. In the days before the prayers, you could tell she was struggling with something. The next day it looked like a huge burden had been lifted.

I had always heard about God's grace and forgiveness, but up until being involved in this experience, I hadn't actually seen it. This experience has allowed me to see it. I was glad that I was able to be there for Deb and help her through her period of depression, even though at times I didn't exactly know how to help. I knew I wanted to be there and provide support. I just hoped that I could provide what she needed to make it through such a rough time in her life.

I have learned a lot about praying with someone else. It really feels like you accomplish something and it is much easier to remember everything from the prayer session, both during and afterwards. It is nice to know that through our prayer sessions, we can help others.

Deb, you have an amazing ability to forgive.

Do to others what you would have them do to you.
Luke 6: 31

When you stand to pray, forgive anyone against whom you have a grievance so that your heavenly Father may in turn forgive you your faults.
Mark 11:25

Bear with one another; forgive whatever grievances you have against one another. Forgive as the Lord has forgiven you.
Colossians 3:13

In place of these, be kind to one another, compassionate, and mutually forgiving, just as God has forgiven you in Christ.
Ephesians 4:32

Points to Ponder:

Is there someone in your life that you need to forgive? What's holding you back? Pray for the Lord to assist you in forgiving someone today. The grace you receive from taking this step is indescribable.

If you are having difficulties moving forward with forgiveness, offer it to the Lord. Pray for strength and allow Him to assist you with your burden. He will not let you down if you put your trust in Him.

A Note on Grace and Forgiveness

In church on April 23rd, we had a priest visiting from another parish. It happened to be Divine Mercy Sunday. His homily was on forgiving others and how powerful this grace is. He also talked about God's mercy and how the death and resurrection shows us the incredible strength of this mercy. The priest asked us to reach out with this knowledge and look for individuals who are looking for that mercy and to show them that way to ask for forgiveness and accept Jesus' heart. As the priest gave this homily,

I not only thought about individuals that I thought I may be able to help, but I also thought about my own prayers of forgiveness and how I had truly forgiven the individuals who had done the most harm in my life. So many times, Ben and John had questioned how I could forgive the individuals who had raped me and if they had been sitting next to me in the pew on Divine Mercy Sunday, I would have turned to them and said, "that's why."

Ben, Deb and P.J. at a special event the day after completing the process of forgiveness.

CHAPTER TEN

Medjagorge

After Lisa realized that I was seriously making major changes in my life and that I had truly integrated the work of *The Miracle Hour* into my every day life, she introduced me to a book titled *Medjagorge: The Mission*. The book is written by Wayne Weibel. Mr. Weibel was a Protestant man and a journalist. At one point in his career, he was doing research on all of the happenings at Medjagorge. While he was doing his research for his work, he received a message of his own regarding the work that God wanted him to do as it pertained to Medjagorge. Lisa told me to read the book and just listen to what it had to tell me. She said that the book had totally changed her life and she was convinced that it would probably change my life too. My first reaction was something like, "do you know how many books I have on my reading pile?" She said she understood but that she really thought I should read the book. She was quite convincing. Needless to say, I finally found some time to begin reading the book as I was preparing to take a work related trip. I will preface the rest of this by stating that yes, this book has not only changed my life, it has really given me the passion to continue moving forward in this journey.

I started reading the book the week before I was scheduled to attend a conference in San Diego. I didn't have a lot of time, but I had read enough of the book to know that I would continue reading it. It was definitely difficult to put down. As I was on the flight from Minneapolis to San Diego, I began reading the book again. As I was reading, I began feeling the Holy Spirit energy flowing through my body. Now, I had enough experience at this point to know that when this energy begins flowing through my body, it either means I am supposed to be praying over someone or I am supposed to be paying attention-something important is going to happen. My intuition was telling me that I was supposed to be praying for someone. I started thinking to myself. This is crazy. I am in the middle of the airplane, reading this book and I have Holy Spirit energy flowing through me that I think is meant for someone. Forget it. I continued reading. But then His voice came into my head. The voice was very clear. It told me that I was supposed to pray with the lady who was sitting next to me. I answered Him back that I thought it was way too "out there" and that I couldn't possibly pray with a stranger like that. She would probably think that I was nuts. I continued reading. As I flipped the next page, there was a part about God giving us strength and courage to do the things He asked us to do. The voice came back again, telling me to pray with this woman. I told Him that I would only do it if He gave me an open door. I was absolutely petrified about this. Not 30 seconds later, she reached over and said, "tell me about that book you're reading." My jaw dropped. I looked at her and said, "are you a spiritual person?" She told me she was. I told her that I didn't want her to think I was crazy but that God wanted me to pray with her-right here, right now. He had a message for her. Immediately, tears came to her eyes. They also came to my eyes. I reached for her hands. As I took them, I told her that I was going to open myself up to His words and what He wanted her to hear. I also said that it might not make any sense to me but that I would say it as I received it. I closed my eyes and opened myself for God's word. I honestly don't remember anything that I told her at this point. They were God's words, not mine. These words were meant for her, not me. At the time, most of it didn't make any sense to me at all, but it definitely made sense to her. I was absolutely in awe. How could this be happening? What was going on? As I finished, she just sat there looking at me with tears streaming down her face. How could you know all these things you just said to me? I told her that I didn't—the words were all from God. She kept thanking me and I told her not to thank me but to thank Him. It was His work—He was the one who should be receiving the praise. As we chatted a little more, I told her that there were a few more things that I was supposed to let her know. I shared those with her and then I told her that God was asking me to pray a special blessing over her neck. I did as I was told and later found out that she had just had surgery on her thyroid. It wasn't the first surgery she had on it, either. It was a recurring situation. I will probably never know God's total will in having me pray over her neck, but I was happy to answer His call. He knows what his intention was. As I look back and think about this, something else sticks in my head. As all of this was going on, it was as if no one else on the plane noticed. Time was standing still. A moment of time froze so that God could accomplish His work. Another interesting thing is that I was flying with two of my colleagues. Normally, we would have sat closer together, but for some reason on this flight, we were all in three totally different areas of the plane. One could argue that this was coincidental, but I would argue that God wanted me available to help this woman at this time and the fewer potential distractions, the better. Once again, He had a plan.

The book continued to speak to me in a big way. Throughout the trip, I continued to read the book. I finished the book on the plane trip home. Once again, I received a message during the flight. There is a last section in the book, where there is a time for reflection and one to think about how that book can be used to either accomplish God's will or speak to the person reading the book. As I was doing this reflection, I had the very distinct feeling that I was supposed to give the book to the gentleman sitting next to me.

I started striking up a conversation with him. We chatted about many different things, but eventually, we got onto the topic of spirituality. He told me that he used to attend church fairly regularly but that he hadn't been going as often. He knew that he needed to make a change in his life and he knew that he was also getting stagnant in many things but he just wasn't sure what he should be doing. I started talking about some of the changes that I had been making in my life. He began asking me about the book I was reading. I told him about it and the impact it had been having. I also told him that I felt God was leading me to give him the book. He got this interesting look in his face. It was a combination of surprise but also a look of relief. He kept insisting on giving me money for the book. I told him that I wouldn't take a dime. I said the best gift you can give me and God is to read the book, put its concepts into practice and then pray about the next person to whom you should be giving the book. That seemed to make sense to him. He accepted the book with the promise that he would read it and he would listen for the voice that would tell him where to go with it next.

The book continues to work in many ways. Each time I have an opportunity to talk about the book, I do. When someone talks about Mary, I bring up the Medjagorge books. There are actually several books by Wayne Weible on this topic. One of my new favorite books relating to Medjagorge is written by Father Richard Beyer. This is a daily devotional book based on the messages that Our Lady has given at Medjagorge. The thing that I enjoy the most about the devotional book is that it contains the message, reflection about the message, and scriptural passages related to both. I find that my day just doesn't feel complete without taking time to read from this book.

I still haven't had the opportunity to meet Wayne Weible, but I know when I do, I will thank him for following God's call to write these books and do his important work. It is not always easy to do God's work and sometimes when we do, it can present trials in our lives. The good news is that by doing God's work, we are pleasing Him and we are helping others in the process. For that, I praise His name every day.

There is one more Medjagorge story I want to share with you. It hadn't been too long after I had finished reading the book and I was at a Mass that I normally don't attend. I was sitting in the back of church, which is also not normal for me. There was a couple standing next to me. I don't know that I've ever seen them in church before. After returning from Communion, I had the very distinct feeling that I was supposed to pray over them and that God would give me the words He wanted prayed over them. I started doubting this call but immediately heard God's voice reminding me that He would give me strength and courage. I reached out to them and asked them if they would mind if I prayed a special prayer over them. I told them that I felt God was asking me to pray something special for them. They looked at each other and said sure. I placed one hand on each of their backs. I opened my thoughts and asked God for the words. As always, the words were there. To this day, I don't remember what they were, but it was apparent that it made sense to the couple. They thanked me many times and I kept telling them to thank God and give Him the praise. Once again, this reminded me that God may call on me when I'm least expecting it, He will give me the strength and courage and He has a plan that needs human beings to intercede for Him. It is through us that He is able to accomplish His work. I feel so grateful and so blessed that he has chosen me to help intercede for Him. I still feel so unworthy, but I would never want to turn my back on Him again.

Seeing his mother there with the disciple whom he loved, Jesus said to his mother, "Woman, there is your son." In turn he said to his mother, "Woman, there is your son." In turn, he said to the disciple, "There is your mother." From that hour onward, the disciple took her into his care.
John 19: 26-27

When Elizabeth heard Mary's greeting, the baby leapt in her womb. Elizabeth was filled with the Holy Spirit and cried out in a loud voice: "Blest are you among women and blest is the fruit of your womb. But who am I that the mother of my Lord should come to me? The moment your greeting sounded in my ears, the baby leapt in my womb for joy. Blest is she who trusted that the Lord's words to her would be fulfilled. Then Mary said: "My being proclaims the greatness of the Lord, my spirit finds joy in God my savior, For he has looked upon his servant in her lowliness; all ages to come shall call me blessed. God who is mighty has done great things for me, holy is his name; His mercy is from age to age on those who fear him.
Luke 1: 41-50

Together they devoted themselves to constant prayer. There were some women in their company, and Mary the mother of Jesus, and his brothers.
Acts 1: 14

Hail Mary

Hail Mary, full of grace, the Lord is with Thee
Blessed are you among women
and blest is the fruit of your womb
Holy Mary, Mother of God,
Pray for us sinners now
And at the hour of death. Amen.

Points to Ponder:

What is your relationship with Mary, the Mother of God?

Do you pray the Rosary?

Have you read about Medjugorje?

CHAPTER ELEVEN

A New Rape Victim

As I stated earlier, the Holy Spirit began working in some incredible ways and there was an experience that really confirmed it with me. I heard about a friend's daughter who had been raped. I immediately started getting the Holy Spirit energy working through my body. This always happens when I know I am supposed to be paying attention or that I have a purpose with what's going to be said. As this person was talking, I realized that I knew the mother of the girl. I had a very strong sense of knowing I should call this mother. I decided to talk with Ben and Jamie first to get their opinion. I wasn't sure that I was at a point where I could be talking with other people yet. Ben and Jamie both thought it would be good for me and it could actually help me heal. I prayed about it all weekend and on Sunday night, I picked up the phone. I identified myself and then asked the mom if she was a spiritual person. She said yes and started crying a little. I told her that I felt directed to call her because her daughter and I had shared a similar experience. The mom started crying. She then told me that my call had been an answer to her prayer request. She said she had been praying for a sign from God to know that He was still with them. That request had just taken place in the last couple of days and I called—answering her request from Him. She told me that the call was also giving her hope. She knew that if I could heal and be the person that I am now, she thought her daughter could do the same. We agreed that we would keep in touch and I was willing to pray with them or do whatever they needed within my capacity for healing. About ten days later, I had a strong urge to e-mail the mother. Again, the Holy Spirit energy was flowing through my body. I sent a quick note just letting her know that I was thinking of her. She e-mailed me back telling me that God was definitely working through me to reach her. Again, she had been praying for a sign because a death had happened in their family the previous evening. She said that my e-mail had renewed her faith and that she definitely knew her prayers were being heard and answered. How else could we explain the timing of my call and e-mail? It wasn't me- it was God working through me. The mother and I have continued a small dialogue via e-mail. When the time is right, I am sure we will meet face to face. I continue to pray for this family for healing. I especially pray for this young lady, who has experienced the horrors of rape and will forever carry it with her. I hope she is able to learn from my experience and that she doesn't have to live in darkness for as long as I did. If this book even helps one young adult, it will be worth every minute it took to write it.

CHAPTER TWELVE

John

"A Man of Nature"

As P.J. was preparing to move to a new town, I began praying for God to bring someone else into my life that could help on the team and support me in many of the ways that P.J. did. I had a spark of an idea after a kayaking course one night. It was a simple thing but yet there was a strong impact from it. A colleague and I had taken a kayak course offered at the Rec Center. One of the instructors was John. I had met him before but we never really had the chance to talk. At one point in the course, we had to learn a self-rescue. I was struggling with this immensely. The other instructor informed me that I didn't have to do this to complete the course. I was pretty determined and wanted to keep trying. I think John saw the determination but also knew I needed help. He stayed right with me and talked me through every single step of the rescue. He then held onto my hand until I was safely in the kayak and able to complete the rescue. His eyes never left mine. He said at one point—"you knew I wouldn't let you give up." I had a thought that maybe, just maybe he would make a great addition to the team. I didn't know him very well, so I knew I would need to get to know him more before making that final decision. The opportunity came a couple weeks later.

One day, I had a couple of hours in between shifts at work. I decided to go walk at the Rec Center. As I was walking, I spotted John at the rock wall. We started talking right away. I felt an immediate connection. He had some things going on and I sat and listened to him for a while. We agreed that we should meet for coffee at some point. I knew at that point that he would be the next person on the team. I couldn't put my finger on it, but I had the feeling of a soul connection. It was almost like looking at my inner self through someone else. I also knew that he verbally processed just like I did so he would understand my need to talk things through. I also picked up his need to feel appreciated and loved. Again, two of the things I identified that I needed too. I really had the feeling that this was the start of something very important.

It took a couple weeks, but John and I were eventually able to get our coffee appointment set up. It was a phenomenal meeting. John shared things with me that he had told very few people. He later told me that he felt as if he had been talking to an angel. He said that he didn't feel judged and he felt extremely comfortable. I felt comfortable talking to him too. I felt as if I had almost an instant trust bond with him. Given my issues with trust, this was particularly important. I remember at one time thinking that when we both talked with each other, it was almost like two souls talking together.

A week after our coffee appointment, John and I had the opportunity to have a very in-depth discussion and our first prayer session together. After John had shared some of his inner most secrets, I asked him if he wanted to pray together. He said he did. I did a blessing and protective prayer from *The Miracle Hour* before we started. It was a very nice prayer session. We both felt the energy of the Holy Spirit and John was able to both forgive others and himself for things that he had not even let himself talk about. It was a pretty incredible experience for both of us. By the time we were done, we had spent several hours together and we were emotionally exhausted. I was so grateful to God for bringing John into my life and I knew that this was just the start of a wonderful relationship.

After this prayer session, John headed to his parent's home for the Christmas break. Throughout the break, we kept in touch with text messages and phone calls. It was amazing how I would get a message from God to text him something and it was exactly what he needed to hear at that time. Some of the most profound messages had to do with rebuking evil spirits and the specific ones that he needed to rebuke. Being a part of this experience was incredible. It proved to me once again how powerful God can be when we simply let Him work through us.

Upon returning from Christmas Break, John and I continued to develop our relationship. One night, I received a call from John. It was about 1:00 in the morning. I asked him what was wrong. He said that he had just broken up with his girlfriend whom he had dated for over a year. I asked him if he wanted to come to our home and talk, which he did. We spent the next five hours talking and praying. It was a prayer session that truly impacted every part of my body. It was as if the Holy Spirit were reaching out to every part of my body to be able to reach John and help him through the difficult time. The next day we spent many hours talking and texting. That evening, we were scheduled to pray. John asked me if I would call Ben and see if he would come too. John, Ben and I met together to pray. After some basic prayers, we all prayed the Rosary together. It was the first time I had prayed the Rosary with either of them and the opportunity to pray it all together was such a blessing. This experience touched my heart and opened the door for God in such an incredible way for all of us. I also felt that it was a good experience to have the three of us praying together. I really cherish this memory and the prayer moments that it provided.

As is often the case, when satan knows that you are trying to get closer to God, he tries to get in the way. This happened with John. A few days after the breakup with his girlfriend, John began to detach. In fact, he detached so much that he wouldn't respond to phone, e-mail or text. I was so frustrated. We were leaving for vacation and I didn't feel like there was any closure at all and I was very concerned about where John was spiritually and emotionally but I couldn't get him to respond. Finally, as we were nearing the end of our vacation, I received an apology text from him. Once I got back to Bemidji, I really wasn't sure what to do. That evening, I received another apology text but he also let me know that he was in a bad space. He said that he hadn't fallen into any of his previous behaviors but that his head was just so full of stuff that he needed some space. What I couldn't seem to understand was that he couldn't communicate this to me while I was gone on vacation. I had spent many hours worrying about him and that's all he would have needed to tell me. Needless to say, I decided that the best thing to do was to give him space. That Tuesday, I happened to run into him at the Rec Center. I know he was trying to avoid me. Not because I think he really didn't want to see me but probably because he didn't know what to say or how to ask for what he really needed. I decided to approach him. When he started by saying how busy he was, etc. I just stopped him and said, "listen—are you just asking for space?" He let me know that he was. I told him that it wasn't a problem. I was happy to give him space if that's what he needed. It was almost as if he didn't believe me. I told him that I cared enough about him that I was willing to give him all the space he needed. I didn't care if it was 1 day, 1 week or a month. I told him that all I hoped was that he would continue to look to God for the guidance and through asking God for that guidance, he would be able to find the peace and comfort that he needed to be able to move forward in his life. He seemed very relieved but I could still tell that he felt a lot of guilt and pain. I knew I would have to be the one to back away for a while so he had the opportunity to work through these things on his own. I also knew that if I gave him the space, he would eventually return. Our team had been talking about doing a dinner on the following Sunday. I had told Jamie and Ben that it would probably be best if we left John alone. They both felt that if the opportunity came up where one of us ran into him that we should invite him to come to dinner and that's where we left it. Amazingly, on Saturday, I ran into him again. I still found this bizarre because on both of the days that I ran into him, they were normally times that I didn't work out and they were also normally times that he didn't work and yet on these particular days, he had a reason to be there. He told me later that he knew I was going to be at the Recreational Center and he was actually nervous about seeing me because he still didn't know what to say to me. I told him to always remember to turn the conversation over to God and the right words would come. Needless to say, after talking for a while, I did invite him to dinner and he agreed to come. That Sunday night was very good for everyone. It was good for us to connect again and it was good for John to be a part of a fun night and not have the intensity of the deep discussions. We also learned a very good lesson, which is that we may have some hard times, but we will work through those times and knowing that the core foundation and reliance on God is there is extremely important. By having this core foundation, we always have something to fall back on. I was also encouraged to know that he hadn't gotten back with his girlfriend and that he really was trying to take a step back and look at everything in his life. From that point forward, we seemed to be able to find a much better way of working together.

As John continued to heal himself, he also became a much stronger source of healing for me. For example, one day during Lent, John called me and asked me if I wanted to meet him in the Chapel to pray. I asked him if he wanted to pray together or individually. He said that he wanted to pray individually, but he thought it would be cool if we were both praying at the same time. I did meet him and it was an incredible experience. We both did our own prayers simultaneously. The really cool thing was that at the end of my prayers, I had tears streaming down my face. There wasn't really anything wrong, but the tears kept coming—literally streaming right down my face. John asked me what was going on and why I was crying. I told him that I honestly didn't know. He just sat there with me while I let the tears stream down my face. I shared with him a few of the thoughts that had been going through my head and he just listened and looked at me. I don't think I've ever seen him look more beautiful than he did at that moment. He had so much compassion and understanding in his eyes. As he got ready to leave, he gave me a big hug. As he took me in his embrace, he said, "don't worry, I have on a waterproof jacket." That just struck me as so funny. I sat there laughing and crying at the same time. It was quite a moment. I also called on John one evening to help me with a healing prayer session. John and I had actually had a bit of a challenge that day with a major misunderstanding in communication. For some reason, though, I had the feeling that he was supposed to help me with this session. I left him a message asking for his help and he said he would. When he entered the room, I knew he was hesitant because he and I had not totally cleared the air but yet he answered the call to come. This was very important to me. As we worked through the prayer session, especially the prayers of forgiveness, I could feel him forgiving me on the spot. I kept hoping that he, too, would feel my forgiveness. His strength and support for me as we did that healing session were very important. There were moments when I knew I needed more of his energy and as if he was reading my mind, he would change his hand position of the way he was supporting me and I had what I needed. As he and I debriefed the prayer session, I told him that he was definitely a source of the Holy Spirit in prayer and that when I prayed with him, I knew that the Holy Spirit energy flowed freely. I knew this was important because having that strength in intensive healing sessions is extremely important.

One more incredible experience that John and I shared was laying his dog Mac to rest. Mac was a great dog. I met him when John brought him to Bemidji. Mac always had a dog smile on his face. His tongue would hang over to the side of his face and his tail was always wagging. He makes me smile just thinking about him. Unfortunately, he got very sick in Bemidji. There were several things that had gone wrong including Lyme's disease. He got so ill that John had to make a decision regarding putting him to sleep. It was one of the toughest decisions he's ever had to make. Ultimately, he decided that it would be best to put Mac to sleep. He called me afterwards to see if I would be willing to go with him to bury Mac. I told him it would be an honor and privilege to go with him. John and I drove to a special place in the woods and hiked to the spot where John wanted to bury Mac. We dug the hole and then sprinkled it with holy water. We placed Mac in the grave and said special prayers for him. I gave John some time alone with him while he said goodbye. It was such a hard time. I also realized how important my relationship with John was. I knew that there wasn't anyone else he would have asked to go with him to bury Mac. I knew he either would have done it alone or called me. I can't explain how much this touched my heart. I remember John telling me that if I ever doubted how much he trusted me or cared about me that I should come out to the place where Mac was buried and I would remember. I can honestly say that I did go out to the woods a couple of times to remember because we definitely had some challenges down the road and I needed to remember in my heart how much he did care for me, even when there were times that his actions didn't communicate that to me.

One very important lesson I have learned through my relationship with John is how important it is to turn conversations and actions over to God—especially when one is feeling insecure, vulnerable or doubt. It is so easy to take these negative feelings and have them continue to get even more negative rather than turning it around into something positive. Since both John and I have a stubborn streak within us, it is particularly important that we turn these things over. What has often started as a small misunderstanding for us has often become something very big that escalates way out of control. If either one of us would have turned the conversation over to God, it probably wouldn't have been such a problem. John would point out that it is through having these types of experiences that we have both been able to be stronger with each other and have actually made the foundation and commitment even better. Yes, he is definitely right. God presented these opportunities to us to that we could increase our trust in one another and also learn to fully rely on God for strength and wisdom in these types of circumstances.

The trust in this relationship continued to be challenged. In May of 2006, John left to take a job in another community. Our plan was to keep in touch and support each other as much as possible. Unfortunately, John leaving this environment ended up presenting another set of problems. Returning to his hometown meant returning to some of the baggage that existed in John's past. It also meant being away from his support team that he had developed in our community. He and I communicated somewhat by phone and text messaging, but I could tell that something was wrong. I could feel that he was not doing the things he needed to do, but he was starting to slip. It became more and more difficult to reach him in conversations. His text messages were vague and I knew he was trying to hide. When we did talk, there were always excuses for why things weren't going right. I finally sent him a text and told him he needed to make a choice. He needed to commit to God and commit to this team or I would have to let him go at this point. His negativity was really starting to bring me down and I knew I couldn't do God's work if this continued to happen. He responded by phone to that call and I felt like we had at least somewhat worked it out. The next day, I had an incredibly strong sense that I needed to drive to see him. It wasn't just a little feeling, it was a very strong feeling, like he was in serious trouble. I made the decision to drive and see him. This wasn't an easy decision. It meant driving 4.5 hours there and back, knowing I had presentations to do the next morning in my class. I really didn't feel like I had a choice, so I went. I had sent several texts on my way to his house and I had also left a phone message. I couldn't figure out why he wasn't responding to me. As I pulled up to his house, I saw him getting ready to leave. He seemed surprised to see me and he was cold. He told me he was going fishing with his brother. I told him that I'd be happy to leave but I did request to use his bathroom before I headed on the road again. After using the bathroom, I met John's mom and she and I had a nice chat. John had started to soften a little and asked his brother if they could go fishing another time. Of course that was fine with him, so John took me on a tour of his town. I sat and listened so he could talk and I could try and figure out what was going on with him. It took about two hours to get to the John that I knew and was a part of this team. Once he started talking, I realized how much he had really changed since leaving. He shared with me that I was one of the only individuals that he could really talk with and that he was just really struggling with a lot right now. We decided to go to dinner and continue our discussion. While at dinner, I checked my phone and saw that John had sent me a text message but it hadn't come through on my phone earlier. As I started checking it, I could see the expression on John's face change. The text basically told me to give him a break.

He had sent this while I was on route to his house. Fortunately, I hadn't seen it on my way, or I would have turned around and not even gone to his house. I started tearing up at the dinner table. He started apologizing. I told him that I just didn't understand what was going on with him and why he was treating me like this. He realized that the message was evil and couldn't believe he had sent it. I just didn't know what to think and I couldn't believe that someone whom I had trusted so much as well as someone I had helped so much would treat me like this. I was almost in a state of shock. We finished dinner and he took me back to my car. I said a quick prayer with him before I left. I really wondered when I left if I would ever hear from him or see him again.

As always, God has His plan for each of us. John and I talked briefly the next week but in the call he basically told me he needed space. It was a very difficult phone call. I knew that giving him space this time really meant letting go. It didn't mean I couldn't forget him or that I wouldn't listen, but I had to let go and let God's plan for John take place. This meant that I had to let go of my expectations and my own needs for John on this team. This also meant accepting the fact that John may not be a future part of this team. I honestly didn't know where it would go. I remember talking with Ben about it one night. Ben told me he hadn't given up on John. I told Ben that I hadn't given up but that it was really going to take a lot before I could trust John and put 100% of my faith in him as a team member and someone on whom I could rely. After about 4 weeks of not speaking at all, I sent a prayer request to John. He did respond to this. After 5 weeks of not speaking, I decided to make one more phone call as I felt God was calling me to do this. I had a very strong sense that John was under a satanic oppression and I knew immediate action needed to be taken before it got worse. I called upon the *Our Lady of Chandra* prayer group to begin intensive prayer and I also began offering daily Masses for John. I was doing anything to get him released from the oppression. I started to see glimpses off hope. I could actually feel the burdens being lifted from him as he continued to move towards Christ's light. I was once again reminded of the incredible power of intercessory prayer. I know it worked for me and now it was working for someone else. John and I started to communicate again. He started reaching out and began taking action to move in the right direction. This was an incredible step for him. We should never give up on people. We can always keep praying for them. Sometimes it takes a long time for something to happen, but it's in God's time. He has a plan for each of us and we never know how that plan will be used—but He does and if we have faith in that, He will take care of the rest. God is so good, isn't He?

John's Corner:

In my short 22 years of life, I have had a few experiences that I am still lucky to be alive to tell about. I have had shortcomings that have changed my life in so many dynamic ways. The question is which experiences have made a difference and changed me and which have left a scar.

To start, I am going to explain the reason I came to write this. I grew up in a normal family: two amazing parents, an awesome sister and the best brother a guy could ask for. I have a family I can always trust and know they would never going to let me down no matter what I do or what I say. In some parts of my life, it was almost like I was trying to break their spirit with the things I would do. I was the captain of the football and baseball teams; president of the science club and art councils and voted onto the Homecoming Court. I can say I was a "popular" kid. I had friends to spare you could say or I would have thought. So what did it come down to? It came down to my choices and my actions. I was not acting as myself but as a follower—so I would be liked by everyone else. Drugs, sex and alcohol were common in my everyday life during my early years until I went to college.

So what did it take for me to change my lifestyle? It took a true friend. It took someone who knew absolutely nothing about me to give me a chance—a chance to be myself using nothing as a mask. When you can look into a person's eyes and laugh, smile, cry and feel what they are feeling, you have a gift that not everyone encounters in their life. This is a gift from the heart and soul that you cannot touch but only feel. This is a kind of feeling I had never had before and it made my spirit absolutely come alive and spread its wings to the world, just waiting for the wind to pick me up. I no longer had anything to hide from anyone and now only something to give. So what do you give back? That's not even the real question because it is not just a "give and take" kind of relationship; it is truth, honesty, reliability, love, confidence, respect, care, faith, fullness and everything else that your soul holds deep. Notice not one of these traits can be touched. You can give them but they cannot be touched because they are held in your heart and only you have the key to open that up. So, I met the first ever true friend and he was taken from me in an instant, with no goodbye.

After he was taken, thoughts came through my head of going back to my old self and cover my problems with any kind of mask that I could find. But that is not what I did. All I could do was hold on to that which I had received and try to find that in others. Number one, you cannot match anyone or anything because we all have our individuality. I soon found that out. So, I went on with the beautiful traits that I had absorbed from a true friend and I let them flow through my life blood, now having those traits actually be qualities of mine but not wholly changing my person.

It was like starting back at square one but with the kind of love everyone needs to experience. It gave me confidence to be my own person and to make my own choices. I noticed for a while that people were not attracted to the person that had confidence and wore their life on their sleeve. It is hard for people to see this kind of openness and accept it with arms wide open. My truth and heart actually scared people away. They did not want to see the inside of someone's soul. It's frightening.

Three years later, someone decided to come into and experience my soul. I do not know whether it was out of curiosity or openness but either way, it was very real and very exciting. Just for a person to try and reach my soul like only one other person had done in the past was incredibly uplifting. How, then, do you know whether someone like this is for real? It's in their words, their eyes, their actions, their smile, their everything. This kind of friendship was almost instantaneous. Friendship does not always come in leaps and bounds like this. It often comes through long amounts of time spent together, that is, if you are holding things back. I was not holding anything back at this time and neither was she. By this time, you may know whom I am talking about. Her name is Deb. I want you all to know that when you are reading this book, it is truly from the soul, not any alternative motives--nothing but pure and spoken truth.

John and Deb out for a bike ride.

Everything God created is good; nothing is to be rejected when it is received with thanksgiving, for it is made holy by God's word and by prayer.
1 Timothy 4:4

"Amen! Praise and glory, wisdom and thanksgiving and honor, power and might, to our God forever and ever. Amen!"
Revelation 7: 12

Points to Ponder:

Do you have a friend who is in need of Christ's light? Pray for that person now. Turn it to God—He will take care of the rest.

What are the characteristics you look for in a true friend?

CHAPTER THIRTEEN

Return to Reconciliation

Being raised Catholic, Reconciliation was a regular part of practicing our faith. At some point, however, I just quit going. In my mind, I figured that there was no way that God would forgive me anyway and since I was on such a horrible path of destruction, I really wasn't thinking about it too much anyway. The more I did my *Miracle Hour* book and the deeper I was getting in my spiritual faith, I decided that a return to Reconciliation was in order. I prayed about which priest I should go see as I knew this would definitely not be the 5-10 minute typical confession time. A very interesting thing kept happening. I was continually given the name of Father Joe Richards. Father Joe had been at the Newman Center in Bemidji shortly after the time that we moved to town. I didn't know him well, but I did remember that I always enjoyed him and I had always appreciated his words of wisdom. I tracked down his e-mail and sent him a note explaining my situation. I had no idea what to expect in terms of a response from him. He did respond and said that he would be more than willing to meet with me and share the Sacrament of Reconciliation with me. At this point, I'm not sure if I was more relieved or scared. I was going to have to do this and there was no turning back. I had made myself accountable to someone else now, not just myself. We scheduled a time in January. I asked Father Joe to keep me in his prayers as I was extremely nervous about doing this. When the date in January came, I was a basket case. I was shaking, pale as a ghost and petrified. My hand was shaking so bad when I arrived at Father Joe's house that I could barely knock on the door. His secretary let me in and I sat waiting for a few minutes while they completed their project. Father Joe took me into his living room so we could have a comfortable conversation. I didn't really know where to start, so I tried to pick a beginning point and went from there. I laughed and I cried as well as experiencing a lot of emotions in between. I shared with Father Joe all of the things that I had actually prayed with Ben about. I talked about the people I had forgiven as well as the things for which I knew that I needed to be forgiven. I talked about all of the things that I felt God was calling me to do. I talked about some of the interesting experiences that I had been having and wanting to make sure that this was God working through me and not something else. After a long meeting (it seemed short to me and then I looked at the clock), Father Joe provided me with absolution. I cannot explain to you what this felt like. Once again, I felt this incredible Holy Spirit energy flowing through my body. Some would describe it as God's grace. I felt an incredible amount of peace and calmness, knowing that I had done the right thing.

As I was getting ready to leave, Father Joe told me that he needed to show me something. It was a picture of him consecrating the body and blood of Christ. He told me to look at the picture and let him know what I saw. After a pause, he pointed to a silhouette of the Virgin Mary. I said, "yes, I see it, but you're missing something over here," and I pointed to Jesus' wounded heart and then an image of the Baby Jesus' head. The silhouette of the Virgin Mary was actually looking at the Baby Jesus. Both Father Joe and I started shaking. Major Holy Spirit energy was running through my body. I couldn't believe what I was seeing with my eyes. I asked Father Joe how long he had the picture and he told me that he'd had it a long time. I also asked him how many people he had shown it to and he said, a lot. I said, "now I know why I was supposed to come here today-it wasn't just about my Reconciliation but I was supposed to come here, to your office and you were meant to show me that picture so that I could direct you to Jesus in the picture. All these times you've shown the picture, you've focused on the Virgin Mary but she intercedes for Jesus. She wanted the focus to be on her son but she needed someone to help you see that." We were both so excited, we could barely think. I had to call Lisa on the way home, I was so excited. The following week, I told so many people about that picture. I was so in awe of what it meant. It wasn't just the picture that had me in awe, but also the fact that once again, I had listened to what God wanted me to do and once again, He had a purpose for it. Praise His name!

Since the return to Reconciliation with Father Joe, I have gone several times. Each time, I feel renewed cleansing. Each time, I feel more "pure". I am humbled when I share with another human being my sins—my faults—my shortcomings. We all have them. We are human. That doesn't keep me from striving to do better. I also know that when I make myself vulnerable and share them with someone else, it is a part of my healing and a way of helping me to continue to live a life that is more like Christ. I also know that each time I have gone to Reconciliation, I have felt in a physical, emotional and spiritual sense, God's grace. It is as if an energy flows through my body that wasn't there before. I thought that I might experience this only the first time that I returned, but that hasn't been the case. Each and every time I have returned for this Sacrament, that feeling has been there and I thank God each time for that grace.

I don't know if I can accurately describe the incredible sense of awe that I feel about God's grace. I know that I received this when I prayed for forgiveness of myself and others and I have also seen this in others who are receiving it. It is phenomenal. The uncontrollable tears that just slide down ones face. The smile that one has—again, almost an uncontrollable type of a smile. The overwhelming sense of unworthiness yet such a strong desire to believe and accept. WOW! Sometimes I just sit and stare at the crucifix and I think about how much Jesus loves us that He was willing to give His life for us so that we are able to experience this grace. It is so profound. I also wonder how many people really think about this. I was doing Reconciliation after a Penance Service one night and for the first two minutes, I just sat there with tears streaming down my face. When I could finally speak, I remember telling Father Todd that I just didn't know where to start because I was just having such a hard time accepting and receiving God's grace. I told him that I could understand it with my head but that feeling it in my heart was an entirely different story. At the same time, we talked about God's will and how difficult it can be to do this will even when we know it's what we're called to do. He reminded me of St. Peter and his struggles to follow God's will even when God was standing right there. It was definitely something that I needed to hear at the time. Oh yes, how God often works in mysterious ways. The biggest thing is that we have to be open to not only hearing His voice but also responding to His call. God's grace and forgiveness are two gifts I hope you have accepted in your life. If you haven't, I urge you to accept them. The incredible "freeness" and love of the Lord that comes with them are so incredible. God wants to give you these gifts. It doesn't matter how bad you think your sins are. God can forgive any of them—but you have to ask! Please say YES!

I thank Christ Jesus our Lord, who has strengthened me, that he has made me his servant and judged me faithful. I was once a blasphemer, a persecutor, a man filled with arrogance; but because I did not know what I was doing in my unbelief, I have been treated mercifully, and the grace of our Lord has been granted me in overflowing measure, along with the faith and love which are in Christ Jesus. You can depend on this as worthy of full acceptance; that Christ Jesus came into the world to save sinners. Of these I myself was the worst. But on that very account I was dealt with mercifully, so that in me, as an extreme case, Jesus Christ might display all his patience, and that I might become an example to those who would later have faith in him and gain everlasting life. To the King of ages, the immortal, the invisible, the only God, be honor and glory forever and ever! Amen!
1 Timothy 1:12-17

My little ones, I am writing this to keep you from sin. But if anyone should sin, we have, in the presence

off the Father, Jesus Christ, an intercessor who is just. He is an offering for our sins, and not for our sins only, but for those of the whole world.
1 John 2: 1-2

The Lord said to Moses, "Tell the Israelites: If a man (or woman) commits a fault against his fellow man and wrongs him, thus breaking faith with the Lord, he shall confess the wrong he has done, restore his ill gotten goods in full, and in addition give one fifth of their value to the one he has wronged.
Numbers 5: 5-7

But if we acknowledge our sins, he who is just can be trusted to forgive our sins and cleanse us from every wrong.
1 John 1: 9

I will cleanse them of all the guilt they incurred by sinning against me; all their offenses by which they sinned and rebelled against me, I will forgive.
Jeremiah 33: 8

For you, O Lord, are good and forgiving, abounding in kindness to all who call upon you.
Psalms 86:5

When they persisted in their questioning, he straightened up and said to them, "Let the man among you who has no sin be the first to cast a stone at her."
John 8: 7

Points to Ponder:

Have you accepted God's grace and forgiveness?

Do you believe that you can take all your sins to the Lord and He will forgive them?

What do you think about when you look at the crucifix?

CHAPTER FOURTEEN

Jamie L

"Armor Man"

Have you ever run into someone or seen someone that you just absolutely know you are supposed to be connected to in some way? That is the case with Jamie L. I remember seeing him a couple of times when I was just getting involved in this process. Even then, I felt a very strong connection to him. At the same time, I wasn't sure what it was all about, so I waited patiently for God's direction. In March of 2006, I definitely knew it was time to start doing something. The sign came as he approached me one day in the gym. He spoke a few very nice words to me, but I saw something else. I saw someone with whom I was supposed to pray. I wasn't sure if the prayer was for him, for me or for someone else, but I definitely knew there was supposed to be prayer. I talked with a mutual friend and asked her if she would be willing to mention something to him. She did and it turns out that he, too, was feeling some type of connection or calling. We were moving into a Spring Break time period, so it was apparent that nothing was going to happen right then. I did have a very strong sense one night that something was wrong. The mutual friend and I decided to phone him. He was trying to tell us that nothing was wrong but I called his bluff. I wasn't buying it. He wouldn't talk then, but I did feel that he at least acknowledged that something was going on and knew that I knew it. It wasn't until a couple weeks later that we were able to connect but it happened in a weird way. I had a very bizarre dream one night and the evening that I had it, I definitely felt that it was for him in some way. I ran into our mutual friend that week and inquired about him. She said that he was a little freaked out about a dream that he had. I asked her to describe it. As she did, I just got the shivers. Our dreams matched about 80%. I had never had this happen before. I told her that I definitely needed to talk and pray with him. I knew I was being called to help in the situation. The next day, I had the feeling that I should go to the Rec Center. I knew he'd be there. I did see him and started to talk with him. He initially started trying to tell me that everything was fine but I told him that I knew about the dream. He asked me how I knew about it. I told him that I didn't want to freak him out but that I had basically had almost the exact same dream that he had and it was meant for him. At this point, he started talking with me. We ended up talking for an hour. I knew he needed prayers and I knew I was the one who was supposed to be praying healing prayers for him. We exchanged numbers and we also arranged a time to get together and pray for his healing.

This healing session was different than any others I've done. Most of the time, I have been praying for my own healing and have had others there to provide strength and courage for me. I have basically guided myself through the process and completed the prayers. The other times, the healing has been with people on my team or people I know really well. This time, I didn't know the individual well and I wasn't totally sure what to expect. For this reason, as well as needing strength and courage, I did ask John to help me with this session. I was very glad that I did. It turned out that many of the messages that we heard and prayed about were the same messages that John needed to hear at this point in his journey.

Jamie didn't just leave this prayer session and end it there. He was ON FIRE! He was telling everyone about his experience and he wanted to find a way to spread God's message with more people. He was so on fire, in fact, that he felt a call to do a mission trip in China. As he prayed about it and started going out to talk to people, he kept getting reinforcement signs. He had so many "coincidences" that we both knew God was working through people to help him complete the mission trip. In addition, God was working through Jamie to reach me. I had a few struggles during the time that Jamie and I were working together and Jamie was always right there, helping me through it and providing uplifting words. In addition, I really felt as if God was speaking to me through Jamie. When we would have a discussion and when Jamie would say certain things, I knew it was God's word. Jamie was also very good at keeping me on track and focused. He cut to the chase and made sure that I continued to stay focused on doing God's work. Jamie has felt many times that God is preparing him for something big and I believe it one hundred percent. Another thing is that Jamie knew that he had a role in getting this book done and helping me prepare to do a mission trip to speak about this book and its message. I never doubted that. It's as if God was telling me the same thing too. "Jamie is here to help you accomplish My work." Again, it is another reminder that God uses all things for His purpose. If we are open and willing to do and accept His plan for us, great things happen!

Jamie made the decision to answer God's call to go to China for the mission trip. This was a big deal. It meant going out and fund raising as well as preparing mentally, physically and spiritually for mission work in another country. Jamie, not being one to do things half way, took on this challenge with vigor. In a very short time span, he met with more individuals and church representatives than you can imagine. There were many times that he was able to share his story and there were many times when he had the opportunity to pray with people. Every time he would have one of these visits, he would call me and say, "Deb, God is working!" It was so inspiring to me to see him so committed to doing God's work! It made me that much more committed to seeing my project through to fruition.

Jamie L's Corner:

In April of 2006, God pulled me from the fire. I had a dream in April that scared me like no other dream.

It was a dream that changed my life. In the dream, I am standing on green grass. The grass erupts with fire around me and I do not know what to do. There is fire all around me and I feel there is no way out. As I begin to lose all hope, I am pulled from the fire and land on a patch of green grass. I look back at the fire and can see graves of people burning. I am so scared of the fire that I start to run. My only goal in the dream is to get home (heaven).

When I woke from the dream, I immediately knew what it meant. I was in the fire, and I wanted to go to heaven, but I knew the only way to heaven was through Jesus. He pulled me from the fire.

Correct those who are confused; the others you must rescue, snatching them from the fire.
Jude 1:22

I later came to understand more about the dream, not only did Jesus pull me from the fire, but He would later use me to pull others from the fire. In the dream, I am too afraid to go back in and grab anyone else out of the fire, but with the help of Jesus, I would soon be prepared.

After my dream, I told a couple friends about it, and what a big impact it had on me. I knew the Lord wanted me to be closer to him, but I did not know what to do, or how to know him more. He soon answered this when he brought Deb McGregor-Pfleger into my life. I had seen Deb at the Rec Center a couple of times that year, and on one occasion I gave her some words of encouragement. She works very hard in the weight room and there always seemed to be a glow around her. I knew I would speak to her some day.

Deb and I shared a mutual friend, and this friend told Deb about the dream I had and about the fire. Little did I know that Deb also had a dream the same night about fire, and when she woke up she saw my name. She knew the dream was meant for me. Deb approached me at the Rec Center a couple days later, and although I tried to tell her everything was fine and that I didn't need any help, she was very persistent. After a couple minutes of small talk she looked me straight in the eyes and said, "Jamie, I had a dream the other night, about the fire, and when I woke up your name popped into my head." I was shocked. My mouth went dry, and I was instantly scared again--the way I was when I woke up from the dream. I knew I needed to speak with her.

That Friday night, I met with Deb and another guy named John. We prayed together. The biggest issue I was dealing with was forgiveness. When Deb was praying over me I could feel my heart tightening. The devil did not want me to feel forgiven. After her prayers had been completed, I slowly felt the tightening around my heart drift away. For the first time in over a year, I had been forgiven. There was much work to be done. I felt God's armor protecting me and I needed to live for God's glory.

In a matter of days, God put mission work on my heart. My uncle used to do mission work in China and was able to connect me to the right people. I contacted an organization called ELIC about doing mission work in China. It was 2 days away from the cut off for accepting applications, but I quickly filled out the paper work and was accepted. I had two months to prepare my passport, visa, get all my medical records together, plane tickets together, everything else and raise $3500. I can assure everyone that there was not one time that God did not walk with me. He opened every door that was needed. While preparing to go to China, I witnessed miraculous events, hearts being hardened and softened as needed. He paved the way for me to go to China.

Many times throughout preparing for China, I was not totally reliant on God and I questioned him several times about if I was going or not. One time that brought me to tears was when I was 3 days from going to China. I had purchased my plane tickets and passport on faith, but I still needed to raise $2000 before I would be allowed to leave. I looked up into the sky and I said, "Lord, I do not want to question your authority and I do not want to question my Father, but Lord, am I going to China?" I heard a voice in the back of my head which brought me to tears. He said, "oh ye of little faith. Why do you question the Lord Jesus Christ? There is not one thing that I will withhold from you. There is not one thing you will go without. Now go my son, you have work from Me to do." The next day, I received the money needed to go to China. God is so good!

One person that constantly kept me reliant and helped me to understand God's will in this time was Deb. I remember one conversation we had where she said, "Jamie, it's not about the mission, it's about doing God's will and accepting His will. If this is what is planned for you, then it will happen." It was so true. It was by God's hand alone that I would go.

While in China, I taught English for five weeks. I was able to tell many about the Lord Jesus Christ, however God also showed me that it is not about saying His name to people. It's about showing His love to people.

On the last day I was in China, I prayed to the Lord about returning home. I asked Him to speak to me, because I needed to know what to do when I returned to America. This is what He said, "Jamie. It is by My hand alone that you were pulled from the fire. It is by My hand alone that you came to China to teach and to speak about Me. And it is by My hand alone that you will speak My message to people when you return to America. What I want you to do for Me, Jamie, is to get the word to the ear. Get My word to their ears. I will do the rest. Tell them about Me, and what I have done in your life. I pulled you from that fire, so that you could preach the good news to all creation. I love you my son. Now go, you have work from Me to do. "

Then he told them: "Go into the whole world and proclaim the good news to all creation." Mark 16:15

Everything that I have written is fact. I did not elaborate once about anything that is written. It is by God's hand that I was able to share this message. I will pray for all who read this that I was able to get the word to the ear. In Jesus' mighty name we pray, Amen... Amen...

Whoever loves father or mother, son or daughter, more than me is not worthy of me. He who will not take up his cross and come after me is not worthy of me.
Matthew 10: 37-38

One night in a vision, the Lord said to Paul: "Do not be afraid. Go on speaking and do not be silenced, for I am with you. No one will attack you or harm you. There are many of my people in this city.
Acts 18: 9-10

In the same way, none of you can be my disciple if he does not renounce all his possessions.
Luke 14:33

As you go, make this announcement: 'The reign of God is at hand! Cure the sick, raise the dead, heal the leprous, expel demons. The gift you have received, give as a gift.
Matthew 10: 7-8

Therefore, since we for our part are surrounded by this cloud off witnesses, let us lay aside every encumbrance of sin which clings to us and persevere in running the race which lies ahead; let us keep our eyes focused on Jesus, who inspires and perfects our faith. For the sake of the joy which lay before him he endured the cross, heedless of its shame. He has taken his seat at the right off the throne of God.
Hebrews 12: 1-2

Jamie L. and Deb.

Brothers, I do not think of myself as having reached the finish line. I give no thought to what lies behind but push on to what is ahead. My entire attention is on the finish line as I run toward the prize to which God calls me— life on high in Christ Jesus.
Philippians 3: 13-14

Points to Ponder:

Have you ever felt a call from God to do something?

Did you answer God's call? What did it feel like?

How do you feel when you KNOW you are doing God's work?

Have you ever considered doing a mission trip?

In what ways is God calling you to do His work today?

Section III—The Future

    Jesus answered: "The light is among you only a little longer. Walk while you still have it or darkness will come over you. The man who walks in the dark does not know where he is going. While you have the light, keep faith in the light; thus you will become sons of light."
    John 12: 35-36

CHAPTER FIFTEEN

The Team

So, you've met this incredible team that helped me move from a place of darkness to a place of Christ's light. Isn't it phenomenal how God worked through each and every one of these individuals to reach me so that I, in turn, could make a choice to serve Him and do His work? The coolest part is that He always had this plan. He knew what He was doing. He was waiting patiently for me to get there. That is what amazes me so much about God in general. He loves us, NO MATTER WHAT! When we hurt, He hurts too. When we sin, He stands there with open arms and says—Jesus died on the cross so that these sins are forgiven. You have My forgiveness and grace. Now, please go share that message with someone else. That's all He asks. It seems so simple and yet at times it's so hard. That's because we're human. But, the best part is that from these mistakes and challenges, we learn. God uses them for His good and provides us the opportunity to teach others. Our God is an awesome God and I want to praise His name every chance that I get. I stand ready and willing to do His will—do you? I am grateful for a team that has stood by me at every step of this journey. At times, they were tired, but listened anyway. At times, they were filled with joy and shared that with me. At times, they pushed, knowing it was what needed to happen. At times, they stood in silence, knowing that, too, was part of the learning experience. No matter what, they have been there. I have never experienced a team like this before and I have been on many teams. This team holds a bond that is very unique. Never have I seen a group of people from such different paths form a union that contained unconditional support and love like that which is present in this group. Never before have I seen a group of young adults so committed to helping a woman in her thirties break a barrier that had been built for 20 years. This team has been so difficult for most to comprehend. In reality, it isn't hard to understand at all. This team is God's team. God formed this team and God is at the center of this team. With God at the center, this team is built on love. With the love of God, anything is possible. How else could you explain any of this? I don't know that I want to understand all of it. I just want to live in its presence and know that God has worked in an amazing way and we have all been so blessed to be touched in this way. In my own way, it is a miracle on Earth. Miracles do happen every day and in all candidness, I believe I am a walking example of it. Lord, I praise and thank You for this miracle and pray that I can be an example of You still completing your miracles here on Earth. I praise You for saving my life and I praise You for the way in which You will take even the worst of circumstances and use it for Your good.

This is my commandment: love one another as I have loved you. There is no greater love than this: to lay down one's life for one's friends.
John 15: 12-13

No one has ever seen God. Yet if we love one another God dwells in us, and his love is brought to perfection in us.
1 John 4:12

He who is a friend is always a friend, and a brother is born for the time of stress.
Proverbs 17:17

Wounds from a friend may be accepted as well meant, but the greetings of an enemy one prays against.
Proverbs 27: 6

Two are better than one: they get a good wage for their labor. If the one falls, the other will lift up his companion. Woe to the solitary man! For if he should fall, he has no one to lift him up.
Ecclesiastes 4: 9-10

Points to Ponder:

Have you ever been on a team? How did it make you feel?

Have you considered starting a faith or support team?

Have you ever witnessed a real life miracle?

Ben, Deb and John on the bike path.

P.J., Ben and Jamie at the rock wall for our "team climb".

My husband Stephen - a BIG part of this team.

EPILOGUE

So, where does it go from here? How does one take the experiences they have had and use it to help others and accomplish God's work? In my case, I received the call to write this book and complete a mission trip where I have an opportunity to share this story and along with it, share strength and hope in the love of Christ. What has been amazing to me is how many people have already gotten involved in the project and the book is just being finished. Someone told me that when you are doing God's work, He'll bring people in your path so His work can be accomplished. It is so true. Every time I have continued to turn this project to Him and ask for guidance on the pieces I don't understand, they happen almost immediately. At one point, I was really concerned about publishers, so I prayed about it. Within a week, I had contacts for three different publishers/individuals who could assist me with this part off the project. Each time, I would praise God and thank Him for letting me do His work. It is still so overwhelming to me that He wants me to do His work, but I told Him I would answer His call and He keeps giving me more work to do! This doesn't mean, however, that there aren't challenges along the way. In fact, I can recall several times where I started doubting this project and what I should do with it. It isn't easy to "put yourself out there" and talk about all of these things. In addition, it isn't just a commitment from me, it is a commitment from my entire family. Often times, I would hear a response from someone that would make me start to question this project. I would have to ask myself, is this satan trying to interfere in this project or is God trying to communicate to me through someone else? Most of the time, I would take it directly to prayer and when I did, I always got the same answer, which was, you are being called to complete this book and the mission trip that goes along with it. I told God I wouldn't let Him down and that I would do His work, so even as those doubts sometimes became incredibly overwhelming, I knew that somehow, someway, God would keep me filled so that my strength and courage would remain. Had it not been for the constant flow of God's love and making His presence known, this book never would have been completed. I pray that God speaks to you in a special way through this book.

Glory be to the Father, and to the Son
and to the Holy Spirit
As it was in the beginning, is now
and ever shall be
World without end, AMEN!

Let no one look down on you because of your youth, but be a continuing example of love, faith, and purity to believers. Until I arrive, devote yourself to the reading of Scripture, to preaching and teaching. Do not neglect the gift you received when, as a result of prophecy, the presbyters laid their hands on you. Attend to your duties; let them absorb you, so that everyone may see your progress. Watch yourself and watch your teaching. Persevere at both tasks. By doing so you will bring salvation yourself and all who hear you.
1 Timothy 4: 12-16

Points to Ponder

Is God calling you to do His work? Are you willing to answer that call?

Pray today for God's guidance in how you can accomplish His work. Ask the Holy Spirit to fill you up with the gifts of knowledge and wisdom as you do God's work.

Resources

Medjugorje the Message
by Wayne Weible
Copyright 1989 by Wayne Weible
Available from Paraclete Press
www.paracletepress.com
http://www.paracletepress.com/
or 800-451-5006

Medjugorje Day by Day
By Richard J. Beyer
Copyright 1993 by Ave Maria Press, Inc
Available at Ave Maria Press, Inc. at
www.avemariapress.com

The Miracle Hour
By Linda Schubert
Available at www.linda-schubert.com
Miracles of the Heart Ministries
PO Box 4034
Santa Clara, CA 95056

About This Book

After turning away from God at age 17, Deb lived a life of darkness, away from Christ's light. This book talks about the reason for turning from Christ in the first place, the struggles along the way of coming back to Christ's light and the incredible team of people that God put into Deb's life to assist her in coming to Christ's light from under a dark cloud. This book will make you laugh, cry and jump for joy, often within the same paragraph. Enjoy this conversational style book that is not only a good testament of the grace and forgiveness of Christ but also provides scripture passages and points to ponder that reinforce God's messages to us.

My Reflections

My Reflections

My Reflections